A HERO'S TAIL

John Gaye

Partners in tackling crime

Published by Wood Green, The Animals Charity.
Published 2013
ISBN 9780992606404

Wood Green, The Animals Charity,
66 Lincoln's Inn Fields,
London WC2A 3LH
www.woodgreen.org.uk

John Gaye is hereby identified as the author of
this work in accordance with section 77 of the
Copyrights, Designs and Patents Act 1988.

Text by John Gaye
Illustrations by Nerys Baker

Designed and produced by Graffeg
16 Neptune Court, Vanguard Way,
Cardiff Bay CF24 5PJ, Wales, United Kingdom
Tel: 029 2043 6560
www.graffeg.com

A CIP Catalogue record for this book is available
from The British Library.

Cover image: Inspector Mark Hobrough and Lady
Back cover image: PC Sam Dunstan and Dante

Contents

Foreword by Paul O'Grady

I was touched when I heard of how the dog handlers of South Wales Police wanted so much to do the best for their four-legged partners that they had started A Hero's Tail. It really is such a lovely story of co-operation between two of the biggest animal charities in the UK and a Police Service.

When I read the stories some made me cry, others made me laugh, but one thing was the same throughout and that is the bond and devotion between the officers and their animal partners. They really are animal lovers.

I was delighted to be asked to help and honoured to be part of this story which is all about helping animals. For me as a dog lover, there is simply nothing better.

Thank you for buying this book, your contribution is hugely appreciated.

Paul O'Grady

Foreword

'A Hero's Tail' is a celebration of South Wales Police dogs and their handlers. The stories tell of the bravery, the skills and the dedication of the police officers and their canine partners who play a crucial, intrinsic role in day to day policing.

There is humour, there is courage and there is sheer dogged determination in these stories, modestly told by the officers, which demonstrates the affection and loyalty of the handlers for their canine partners. This has been the driving force behind the officers' desire to improve the facilities at South Wales Police for their four-legged friends.

In a period of austerity, the officers understood that an upgrade to the facilities within the Dog and Mounted sections was unlikely to be met from public funds and so they set about raising the money themselves. This book is the result.

All of the profits raised from the sale of 'A Hero's Tail' will go towards the welfare of the dogs and horses of South Wales Police, with any surplus going to Wood Green, The Animals Charity, who have supported and underwritten this project since its inception.

This is a wonderful initiative and I commend all those who have been involved. The book simply would not be published were it not for the commitment of a wide range of people within South Wales Police together with our tremendous partners, not least the many generous sponsors whose support has made this project possible.

I hope that you enjoy the stories and the opportunity to take a look at the unique relationship between police officer and police dog.

South Wales Police Chief Constable Peter Vaughan
O.St.J, QPM, CCMI

Acknowledgements

This book could not have been written without the active support, encouragement and initiative of so many. At the top of this list must be three people in particular.

Firstly, Inspector Mark Hobrough, officer responsible for the Mounted and Dog Sections of South Wales Police, from whom came the original initiative for this project, and who then drove it forward by identifying and then cajoling, hectoring and otherwise encouraging officers and ex-officers, to make their individual contributions. He also came up with the brilliant title, A Hero's Tail, for the book.

Secondly, Matthew Rees, a volunteer with South Wales Police, who took the idea and then became the driving force and coordinator of everything since. Matthew's enthusiasm, drive and every bit of spare time have been focused for many months on finding the sponsorship, the support and the endorsement from all those whose names follow. In this he has been ably supported by his wife Sian, who has quietly indulged his passion for this scheme, no doubt to the detriment of much of their social life and time together, while turning out to help in so many ways.

And thirdly, PC Mike Newman, who has been the essential link into the Dog Section and who has been involved in this project from the very start. He has given up so much of his own time and effort in working tirelessly behind the scenes to make many logistic necessities happen. Additionally he patiently provided so much expertise, knowledge and active experience to the author (and his wife, Denise, who provided the author with generous hospitality and introduced him to Welsh Whisky).

The team from Wood Green, The Animals Charity have been hooked into this ever since their Chief Executive at the time, Group Captain Dennis Baker OBE, made the decision to under-write the project. But since then, they have provided so much more, not least a massive amount of support and enthusiasm from so many individuals: Clive Byles, Sharon Evans, Emma Jeffrey, Paula Loveday-Smith, Keith Cockram, Sue Ketland and of course Nerys Baker whose wonderful illustrations enhance the stories so well. In this they have been hugely supported by their Board of Trustees led by their Chairman, Celia Waldron.

A particular thank you must be made to Sir Henry Boyd-Carpenter, Wood Green's President, and Lady Boyd-Carpenter who have devoted many hours to proof-reading this book.

The Dogs Trust have provided support in the form of marketing advice from their Marketing and Fundraising Director, Adrian Burder; technical advice from their property team, Matthew Taylor and Paul Wass; and moral support and encouragement from their Chief Executive, Clarissa Baldwin OBE, and their Board of Trustees led by their Chairman, Philip Daubeny.

A Hero's Tail would never have got off the drawing board without the financial support of so many sponsors who so generously have provided the funds to cover the costs of production. Their names appear elsewhere in the book but at the time of going to press the list reads as follows:

Agria Pet Insurance
All Things Wild, Honeybourne
Canon Ltd
Cardiff Castle

Centaur Veterinary Services Ltd

Ceva Animal Health

Miele Ltd

Safe Solutions

The Spirit of Pegasus

Technik Technology Ltd

Veterinary X-Rays

Vet Index Publications

W&H (UK Ltd)

We have been given enormous encouragement by the people of South Wales, who have already generously shown their support of the project at various events, and of course by our guest celebrity, Paul O'Grady, who has kindly written a foreword in support.

We have been so happy with our choice of Graffeg as publishers of the book. Locally based in Cardiff and largely dealing with Welsh issues, they have provided so much more in support of this book than they were contracted to do. In particular thanks to Matthew Howard and his team for all their support and advice.

Our marketing has benefitted enormously by the efforts of Ant Steele and of Nicky Davies, both of whom have given many hours of their free time to the project.

In the South Wales Police Force we have been so fortunate in getting the early and active support of the Chief Constable, Peter Vaughan QPM, who has written a foreword to the book and Superintendant Steve Furnham, in charge of the Operations Support Division, without whose active support not much would have happened and whose considerable enthusiasm has encouraged so many of those involved.

But finally there are the members of the Force who have

done so much work in putting A Hero's Tail together; Sergeant Tina Baxter who, even while recovering from surgery and with her leg in plaster, continued to provide administrative support to the project; PC Emma Viant who, despite being slightly distracted by the arrival of her first child, compiled all the stories in this book and wrote some notable ones herself; Trevor Wallbank, who has created the website and the financial team led by Karen Campbell-Ace.

But above all, there are the members of the Dog Section, going back over some years, who gave so generously of their time to compile the stories. Their names appear above each of the stories, so do not need to be listed here, but there are so many tales that failed to make the book and each and every one involved time and effort in the compiling. Without them it is quite safe to say that the author would have had nothing from which to work. As it was he was spoilt for choice and sadly had to leave so many amusing and interesting anecdotes unwritten.

There will no doubt be names of supporters, sponsors and active participants who have been omitted from this list through memory lapse or through the ignorance of the author. To everyone involved, on behalf of the author and the dogs of the South Wales Police Dog Section – thank you for your support in whatever way it was offered.

John Gaye, May 2013

Introduction

South Wales Police Force covers a huge, and hugely diverse, geographical area stretching from the furthest outskirts of Cardiff in the east to the Gower Peninsula in the west and as far north so as to include the Valley communities in their dramatic mountain surroundings.

The Force is one of the larger police forces in the UK with 3,184 police officers and around 1800 civilian staff to cover 800 square miles (2,074 sq kms). In support of the 'Bobby on the Beat' is an impressive range of technical wizardry and other resources. Not least amongst this support is the Mounted and Dog Section – based in the centre of the Region at Waterton Cross, Bridgend – with its Training Centre, where dogs from many police forces are trained and assessed before being deployed on operations.

Some of the canine skills available are very specialist but the dogs are selected for their natural abilities that have been developed in the various breeds over many generations. For hundreds of years humans have selectively bred dogs to perform certain tasks; some to protect the home and family, others to help hunt for food. In the 21st century these specialist traits have been further developed to assist our law enforcers in their many roles.

All General Purpose police dogs, most of which are Shepherd types (eg German Shepherds and Belgium Malinois), are trained in all aspects of human restraint so they can be deployed in all situations of potential civil unrest. These include a whole range of events: escorting soccer fans to a stadium; dealing with drunks on a Saturday night; controlling large aggressive crowds; disarming and restraining individuals armed with any form of weapon or firearm. These protective roles are all well known by the general public and very often just the presence of a dog can inhibit or discourage bad behaviour.

But these dogs can multi-task. They can follow a human track for many miles through the very worst of conditions and they can detect items, as small as a single key, that have been dropped by a fugitive. Many of the tales in this book will demonstrate the range and depth of their skills.

And then there are the specialist dogs, usually from the traditional gun dog breeds – Labradors, Spaniels or various types of Pointers; dogs which can detect minute quantities of drugs no matter how imaginatively concealed. Sometimes just as important is their ability to sniff out money, as a sizeable stash of unexplained cash can often be used as evidence of nefarious or criminal activities. Others from these breeds are trained to detect explosives and, in an age of constant threat from terrorism, are in regular demand prior to visits by royalty, politicians or any other celebrity, or in places under threat such as airports.

Another rather more macabre skill and one that is a very specialist role is that of the 'cadaver dog' which can detect human remains even in the most demanding situation. You will not find any stories about these dogs; their role rarely leads to any humour but that does not detract from the vital role they play.

Where do these dogs come from? Some police forces use specialist breeders. However South Wales Police generally select their dogs from the huge population of dogs that find themselves, for whatever reason, no longer wanted by their previous human carers. Sometimes they will take dogs directly from their original owners but frequently they can find suitable dogs from a large selection available from rehoming centres, such as those run by Wood Green, The Animals Charity or The Dogs Trust.

The advantage of using these high quality and responsible rehoming centres is that they get a wide selection from which to choose, all of which have been carefully assessed by experienced animal behaviourists before being recommended as being suitable for the various roles of police work. Some of these dogs may have been strays but, much more likely, they will have been handed in by the original owners whose personal circumstances have changed or who have recognised that the dog is just not right for them.

The dogs selected will usually be under 18 months of age as this helps in the training process. Not all of them will make the cut as fully-fledged police dogs and those who fail will usually be found long-term loving homes as family pets.

Once selected as a potential police recruit, a dog will then be matched to a specific handler and they will then go through training together. Unlike the dogs the handlers will not be total novices. Almost certainly he or she will be a highly experienced police officer who at some stage decided to change roles from other police work. There is usually no shortage of volunteers wishing to join the ranks of the Dog Section and, as with their canine partners, not every volunteer makes the grade. Once selected, few officers leave the Dog Section, except eventually on retirement.

So after between 6 to 13 weeks of training, depending on the role, both handler and dog graduate from training school and go onto operations. Most officers have responsibility for more than one dog, customarily one General Purpose dog and one more specialist search dog. The officer now takes on the role of owner/carer for these dogs on a 24 hour, 7 days a week basis. When the officer knocks off work, the dogs go home as well. Although they will have an outdoor kennel and 'run' in the garden, the dogs will become part of that officer's family and frequently when the dog becomes too old or infirm to do its job it will revert to just being a family pet. It is extraordinary how a dog can spend its time on duty exhibiting a massive dislike for everyone other than its handler and then goes home and can be trusted to play with the family. But it is probably not a good idea to burgle that house or threaten anyone in it!

In the South Wales Police Force, each dog has its own purpose built vehicle. The vehicle will have air conditioning for the long hours spent on patrol but when an officer has to leave the vehicle with the dogs inside he will always leave the back doors open to ensure their comfort and welfare. Recently installed, each vehicle now has an alarm system that will alert the officer by mobile telephone should the internal temperature rise above a certain level on the hottest of days.

As you will discover from the stories in this book the dogs are great 'force multipliers', in that their deployment to a scene can often save on manpower or other more technical resources. Thus they save many thousands of pounds of public money as they can usually do the work more efficiently and more effectively.

This is a book to celebrate the police dogs of South Wales Police and their handlers. The stories you will read are all based on true events and, although sometimes locations or the identities of people have been modified or changed, they all originated from the accounts written by the handlers themselves.

The net profits from the sale of this book will go towards the enhancement of the accommodation of the dogs at the Waterton Police Dog Training Centre, which is currently in desperate need of improvement. The surplus, if any, will go to Wood Green, The Animals Charity, which has supported and under-written this project so strongly from the very start.

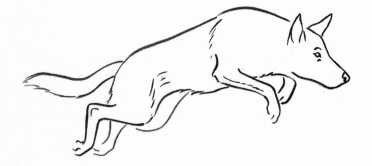

The Tail from the Head

A few words from the officer in charge – Inspector Mark Hobrough.

Inspector Mark Hobrough

When I became Inspector of the Dog and Mounted Section eight years ago, some colleagues asked me why I was joining the department. They actually questioned what this specialist department brought to the Force's overall goals and whether they were expensive resources that were over-valued in a modern crime-fighting era. Personally I had always had an interest in the dogs and had seen at first-hand, as an operational police officer, some brilliant police dog work, often in really bad conditions and frequently in the middle of the night. So I thought I knew a little of what they were capable of, though looking back it was a fraction of what I know now.

On my arrival at the Section it quickly became apparent to me that an incredible amount of fantastic police work was being completed by our handlers and their dogs, most of which was never being promoted properly or receiving recognition in spite of it contributing hugely towards crimes being detected, property being recovered, vulnerable missing people being located, drugs being found and criminals being located, apprehended and receiving punishment. Often none of this would have happened without that police dog and handler involvement. I used to read operational reports from PC Sam Dunstan and her legendary dog Dante and PC Ian Hemburrow and his dog Charlie and they literally made the hairs on my neck stand on edge. Regularly in the middle of the night they were attending what we would all regard as really serious crimes such as burglaries, violent offences, sexual offences and vehicle crime, in all types of weather and across all types of terrain. They were then tracking from crime scenes in challenging circumstances to locate criminals hiding in densely wooded areas and went on to arrest offenders for these horrible crimes. Sometimes the offenders would attempt a foolish struggle and would always come off second best to the dog. I could only imagine the buzz that this must have provided for the officers. Locating such serious criminals with a dog that you had trained from a normal civilian dog must have been just so rewarding. I doubt that they ever slept much at night after such results!

I therefore began compiling a quarterly report detailing the ten best Dog Section incidents of note for each part of the Force area, which I sent out to each area's Senior Management Team to inform them of what had been happening in their area of command and what the dog teams had done to assist them. They clearly had been previously unaware! Suddenly I was having requests from certain senior officers for those reports if they were a few days late in arriving; handlers were having emails and calls of thanks from managers and they even started receiving hand-written letters of thanks from the Chief Constable. Because the managers were now making their own staff aware of these results, the Department's reputation grew and so did general officers' knowledge of the dogs' capabilities; hence they were being called to more and more incidents. Success breeds success I suppose but what is certain was that the dog teams were then, and have always since been, very, very busy and in demand. Internal press and local press began taking interest in particular incidents and events in which the dogs were involved and began running stories on them.

It was the foundations of these excellent pieces of work by dog teams and the subsequent writing up of their operational reports that led us to the content of this book, to which has now been added, substantially, many of the very funny sides of police work with dogs as well as unfortunately some of the sadder sides too.

There are many people who have contributed stories to this book to whom we are grateful but there are also so many other stories that could have been included but we ran out of book space. As the Inspector of the Dog Section some things I'd like to provide from my own experience, in addition to all these tales, have to include: -

When I personally was searching with PC Dick Wiseman and his search dog Joey at the Millennium Centre prior to the Queen's arrival. Joey jumped up on a Chesterfield leather sofa before letting out a half second of urine that managed to saturate the sofa totally. Obviously we cleaned it up but couldn't help wondering whether people might think their posh suits had been starched intensely at the dry cleaners before they attended, such was the strong aroma in the air. This was where Joey earned his nickname of 'Hosepipe Joey'.

On the subject of dogs searching before the arrival of royalty or other VIPs at events, I chuckle at the fact that our visitors must wonder why there are always white hairs on the chairs that they are about to sit on at all the venues that they attend nationally every day. HM The Queen herself has probably had to brush a few off her clothes over the years which means it is just as well she is so fond of dogs.

I recall PS Ian Roderick's infamous General Purpose Dog Kugo – who caused me to dread coming in on a Monday morning to hear about Ian's eventful weekend stories and pending complaints of Kugo chasing horse riders, other dogs, cats and general other wildlife.

Also PS Ian Roderick's search dog Millie who, when searching a route on a cold training day in January, decided to take a dip in a large lake and never return! Fantastically obedient in buildings, she was somewhat challenging outside and ignored Ian's commands to return. Instead she swam across the lake, trotted over two small mountains and into another series of lakes with Ian in hot (or rather cold and wet!) pursuit. He lost Millie over the terrain and feared the worst in the cold weather and water; though, to his credit, he didn't give up searching until it got very late and very dark. Before he resumed his search early the next morning he was contacted to be told that the dog warden had found the dog, which was duly returned – and retired shortly later to become his pet!

Staying on the 'wet dog' theme, an event I will never forget came during the 2012 Olympics. Following a search of the Millennium Stadium on a hot August Saturday afternoon, four of us took our search dogs down to the River Taff to cool them down. Four Springer Spaniels were soon submerged in cool water chasing four tennis balls as we all stood on the river bank and had a few moments of 'downtime' throwing the balls in for the appreciative dogs. All of a sudden one of the dogs decided it wasn't going to play anymore and got out leaving three dogs and four balls. Now it was unknown to the rest of us that PC Steve Sutton's dog 'Sophie' was so ball obsessed that she would not leave a ball behind. She tried and tried, and repeatedly failed, to get the two balls into the gape of her mouth. In this time she totally ignored Steve's calls to come in and soon she was ignoring all of our calls for her to swim to shore. Slowly she and the two balls began to go down river. At one point I confiscated the ball from my own dog 'Lady' and sent her to fetch the extra ball but, as she closed on it, Sophie's growl was enough for her to return to shore empty-mouthed.

By now we were all getting worried as Sophie was showing signs of tiring. As you can imagine with all the screaming of us in our full uniform and dogs splashing about just a bit, a large crowd had now gathered on the bridge and the banks of the river. Steve, who is a 6' 7" tall, ex-Welsh International Rugby player (a little less fit now he is in his mid fifties and certainly lacking a sun tan!), decided there was nothing else for it but to strip to the waist and enter the river after his dog. At first he was only wading but soon it got so deep that he was doing full front crawl after her and to his credit he reached her and swum her back to the river bank, much to the laughter and applause of the watching crowd who thought they had just witnessed an additional Olympic event! Having told her she was a 'good girl' and settled Sophie down (well there was a crowd watching!) it was time for me to send Steve home to have a hot shower and a full change before he returned to work later that afternoon for some stick from his very concerned friends and colleagues.

Steve had over 30 years police service at the time and could easily have retired but had decided to stay on to work for the whole of the Olympics' event and thus leave on a legacy. Well he sure did that! Having most colleagues ask him if he was leaving for a swimming instructor or a lifeguard's job, he also gave me a great story for his retirement speech the following month. I was amazed actually with all those people watching and all those mobile phone cameras that he never made it onto the Internet. He did make it into the local press the next day though – can you guess the title of the article? 'Hero cop risks life to save drowning dog' – it was not. It was 'First unconfirmed sighting of Beluga Whale in River Taff!'

Other funny things I saw that happened during the 40 days of Olympics' searches included PC Carl John's search dog (ironically named 'Chewey') eating the Millennium Stadium

Security Manager's sandwiches on a pre-event search; and PC Kevin Hughes search dog Jack getting stuck between the vertical bars of the gates of a car park as he mistakenly took a short cut, while following his handler, through a gap where his head seemed to fit through frontwards but which then blocked the rest of his body. Just at the point where I thought we were calling the Fire Service to cut the bars he managed to wriggle free for his tennis ball! No harm or injury I should add!

I took on my own search dog 'Lady' from her previous owner, the sadly late but great dog handler Dai Rees who once had a nasty scare with her. Having been tasked to search Cardiff Castle he climbed the 180 feet of the steps of the Castle's 'keep' – Lady ahead of him searching. When he got to the top, to his horror he realised that there was only a four-foot retaining wall surrounding the top of the keep's drop into the moat. There on the wall, was Lady, sure-footed but as busy as could be, running along the top of the wall. Dai gently called her back to come alongside him and put her lead on (and then went and changed his trousers!)

She never changed with me. She still has a propensity to surprise and scare people. I like to run with her on my days off and I have a local coastal path route alongside the beach, free from traffic, where she can run off-lead with me, which she also enjoys. One day however Lady went off course and darted onto the beach to disturb a couple behind some large rocks who were, shall we say, engaged in some activities requiring clearly few clothes! I'm not sure if the man was shocked or angry but I think he had to go home and change his trousers too! No need for police action, though I think my dog had administered the justice and spoilt the moment.

It also can't go unmentioned that in 2012 our own PC Kevin Hughes and his General Purpose Dog Zeena became the first ever Welsh Police Dog Team to win the National Police Dog Trials in Surrey and made us all very proud. They narrowly missed out on retaining their title in 2013 and finished second as we hosted the trials in South Wales. The competition has run for 53 years now, and involves the very best police dogs in the country attending and competing against each other in all aspects of search, location, agility, obedience and criminal work. Only the best get to the event having won their own Force and then their Region's trials on route. The achievement is therefore a remarkable one and Kevin deserves great credit for the effort he has put in to getting Zeena to such a high standard – much of this in his own time.

Operationally, incidents are still happening thick and fast now and only in the last couple of weeks PC Richard Heath and his drugs and currency dog Cracker found the proceeds of a Cardiff bank robbery in a really inaccessible scrub area into which the fleeing offender had thrown it – no doubt to recover at a later date; PC John Johnson and his General Purpose Dog Prince found the still bloodied large knife used at a multiple stabbing in Barry, concealed in the underside of a gutter area which would have otherwise gone unnoticed by human eye; the same team commandeered a lift off a passing van to drive the length of a road to decamp and catch a fleeing burglar in Cardiff; and PC Adrian Lang's drugs dog Swede found a large ball of amphetamine base stuffed inside the head of a Vauxhall Nova gear stick. Now that is what I call a real "gear stick"! The stories in this book are therefore never ending and always evolving and the dogs never cease to amaze us all. I truly believe we have still only scratched the surface of a dog's capabilities and we probably only know 5% of what they can do at the moment.

Unfortunately there isn't room in this book for so many of the other fantastic dog teams over the years and there are no individual stories about so many of them – notably, for me, PS Richie Donovan and his fantastic dog Zac who caught so many prisoners after so many extensive tracks or the late PC Dai Rees and his renowned and revered Doberman Cross Max. I think just their results and reputations speak for themselves and are worth mentioning alone.

So many more dog teams have worked here at the SWP Dog Section over the last 53 years (funnily enough the Section is the same age as the Police Dog Trials) and all have contributed hugely to the development of our dog teams to today's remarkable standards. There are also so many people who work behind the scenes to whom we should also be grateful. These include: Alyson, our Units Administration Clerk; all of our Animal Welfare Officers who care, feed and exercise the dogs based here when officers are sick or on leave; and let us not forget Ginger the Cat who has kept the unit free of mice and rats over the 18 years he has been here. We pass our thanks to them all.

I know how much pride and pleasure they have all derived from their time with the Dog Section and that they will be delighted that the stories they have contributed will result, hopefully, in raising sufficient funds to ensure that we can bring about a total kennel refurbishment for the benefit and welfare of the dogs who made us who we are. Our canine partners, who ask no questions of us, give us continuous loyalty and daily put their lives at risk for us. They are our extremely loyal colleagues and they deserve the best in return. As the now retired PS Alan Hubbard once said to me 'You're only as good as your dog'. He was right.

But finally I feel it most important to express my gratitude to Matthew Rees, a man who has driven this project from the very start, and made it all possible by coming up with new ideas and using all of his contacts to put us in touch with the right people to make this book happen. Matthew is a man who is extremely tenacious and positive in all he does and is so hard working and committed to the cause. He never takes 'no' for an answer, his glass is always half full, not half empty, and it is a pleasure to be in his company. Matthew, you would have made a fantastic Police Dog handler, as you never give up. We all thank you for all you have done to make this book possible.

Trust your Dog

There is a natural tendency in all humans to think that we know better. If a warning light comes on in a car that seems to be working perfectly well the typical first thought is that it must be a faulty light, despite the millions of pounds spent in the development of the car's electronic warning systems.

So it sometimes is with dogs and their handlers. The dog has been selected for its particular skills; it has been trained by experts in developing those skills and tested comprehensively before being allowed to work. Since becoming qualified, regular training and constant assessment by others ensures that the dog's skills are maintained at a high level. Despite all that, at times it is still a natural tendency for a handler to believe their own skills or instincts are greater than their dog's. Hence the handler has to be as highly trained as their dog and must always remember that a dog's powers of smell are phenomenally greater than theirs.

No matter what the dog's specialities are, it is vital that both dog and handler trust each other implicitly. However, sometimes human nature over-rules all that training.

PC Sam Dunstan

It was mid-November and half way through our night shift when I decided to call into Ely police station to grab a cup of tea, not least to charge my own batteries as I was at that stage of the night when every bush, tree, bag of rubbish, gatepost or piece of garden furniture starts to take on human form. I was sitting there chatting to the officers on duty when a call came though that there had been a burglary at an isolated farmhouse in the St Hilary area of the Vale of Glamorgan. I abandoned my tea and ran out to my vehicle where Dante, my very special dog, was curled up in his cage fast asleep.

In those days I travelled everywhere with the sliding glass panel of his cage wide open so he could come through and put his head over my shoulder to watch where we were going. This had the great advantage when speed was vital that he could exit the vehicle with me through my door. He loved to stand with one foot on the passenger seat, the other on the hand brake and he would howl with excitement when the siren was used. This is no longer allowed for perfectly sound safety reasons; I suppose that makes sense but it is not nearly so much fun!

So we set off for St Hilary as fast as I could manage, with Dante in his usual position. On our arrival at the farmhouse we were met by a local officer who explained that the elderly lady occupier had woken up and disturbed four men in her house. Apparently they had taken many precious antique items and some money. The farmhouse was a large detached house, set back from the road along a driveway and surrounded by a paddock and an orchard with a small barn behind it. The farmyard was bordered by hedges that led on to the fields that completely surrounded the property.

I went back to the van, put Dante into his harness, and together we walked over to the front door where we met the owner, a very frail old lady in a long white nightdress. She was, not surprisingly, very upset; she was shaking and her face was ashen white. One of the officers had fetched a coat to wrap round her as she was freezing in the cold of the night. She told me that the burglars had exited through the back door so Dante and I started our search from there.

Dante quickly picked up a scent but all along I was thinking this is going to be a very short track as who in their right mind in this remote area would not have a car parked close by in which to make their escape. But you can never tell with the criminal mind and now we were completely in the hands of Dante. I had, as always, to trust him and his tracking skills implicitly.

Dante turned around and started to track diagonally across the garden towards the hedge line. To my surprise I saw a green baseball cap on the ground. Dante then tracked to the hedge and pushed through a hole into the open fields. As we went through the hole I saw footprints in the mud leading into the field. Dante was on to them.

Dante tracked across the fields, going under barbed wire fences, eventually turning right and cutting diagonally across a large field until we hit a muddy gateway. Dante jumped the five bar gate and had to wait for me to follow. As I climbed over I could see that Dante had found something near the hedge. As I got over the gate I saw he had found an antique trophy, which had obviously been stolen from the house. Dante continued to track across the next field and eventually came to an electric fence. He ducked under it with ease leaving me to jump it for fear of being electrocuted – oh how I hate electric fences. Thankfully it wasn't set very high and I managed to get over without being shocked. Again half way across this field Dante found another piece of property from the house, this time a sporran. This continued for another two fields with Dante finding property from the burglary strewn all across the fields. Things that the burglars probably thought were worthless but to the elderly lady were of significant sentimental value.

Eventually after about a mile Dante turned into a field of cabbages. The smell from the broken foliage was overpowering for me so what it must have been like for Dante I don't know. He tracked across this field faster than he had before and he started to whine. He was getting closer. I knew from experience with Dante that this was his signal.

I was running as fast as I could to keep up with him but with every stride I made I was being pulled forward, over-extending my legs. Eventually Dante came out of the cabbage field and went out onto the main A48 road. Here he stopped suddenly and I saw he had found a bag hidden in the undergrowth containing more items of property from the house. Dante then crossed the road on to the opposite grass verge and turned left. I now saw two males ahead of us come out of the field opposite and walk towards a Renault Clio car parked in a lay-by. By this time a Cowbridge officer had driven along the A48 and pulled up behind the Clio. Dante and I approached the men and I explained to the officer that I had tracked to this location from the farmhouse. The two men were very muddy and quiet and could only say that they were out rabbiting and knew nothing of a burglary. They had with them a small black Lurcher dog, so, on the surface, all appeared to be in order.

However I still knew that we had tracked them from the house to here and I trusted my dog. As we questioned the men, one of them started to get aggressive and abusive, eventually lunging forward to strike the Cowbridge officer. As he did so, Dante jumped forward and bit him on the bottom ripping his tracksuit bottoms off. Needless to say the attack on the officer stopped immediately and both men were arrested. Once interviewed at the custody suite it was found that these two were in a gang of some five men who had set out that night to go rabbiting but had then decided to burgle the farmhouse, thinking it was unoccupied. Their mobile telephones contained photographs of the farmhouse taken from the adjacent fields some days before and also photos of another property nearby. The other men were arrested a few days later after being 'grassed up' by the two arrested on the night. Thankfully all the property stolen from the house, including the money, was recovered.

I often think back to that night and wonder how that poor old lady is today. Whenever I drive past the farmhouse on my way back from Waterton Cross, I think of how afraid she must have been and how it must have affected her life from then on. She must feel vulnerable and helpless and I can only hope that Dante's efforts on the night made a difference to her, knowing that the persons responsible were brought to justice for what they did.

PC Alan Russ

It was mid-winter and in the early morning Swansea was coming to life as the rush hour traffic began to build up and hints of daylight began to appear in the sky to the east. I was monitoring the radio traffic of my colleagues on the local channel as they had identified, and were following, a stolen car being driven in the northern part of the town.

I was en route to the area with my dog, Chase, when I heard that the stolen car had crashed and the two men inside had run off. The officers had managed to arrest the passenger but the driver had run off into the nearby housing estate. It took us just five minutes to join them.

On our arrival I immediately sent Chase to search in the garden of the adjacent house and he started free tracking through all the gardens in that row of houses. It was only a couple of minutes before he started to bark, his 'Number One Bark', which signalled that he had detected a suspect. I very quickly joined him about eight houses from where we had started but things did not seem right to me.

Chase was barking furiously at the council worker who

was part of the team collecting the wheelie bins and emptying them into the dustcart. This was definitely not our man and fortunately he was sensible enough to stand stock-still. I called Chase back to me and apologised profusely to the dustbin man who carried on back to his truck a rather shaken man. We followed him back to the street and headed back to where we had started the search, very disappointed that Chase had made such a fundamental error.

We had only gone ten yards before the bin man called us back. As he had tipped the wheelie bin over the back of his truck our fugitive had fallen out of the bin with all the household rubbish. Despite all the usual smells from a week's rubbish collection, Chase had been right all along in sniffing out our man in the bin. It was me that had failed him, not the other way round. Lesson learnt – trust your dog.

PC Mark Randall

Ynysybwl is a small village just to the north of Pontypridd, deep in a valley and surrounded by mountains and wild countryside. It was in the middle of the night that I was sent with my dog, Ally, to a remote house on the mountainside above the village where a burglary had just taken place.

We were very quickly on the scene and as it was a cold, clear night with a full moon the visibility was excellent and I was confident we would have some success. We set off on foot, with Ally in his harness and on a lead, tracking down the mountainside back towards the village. In the half-light I could make out that the direct route led through a large area of reeds but Ally decided to skirt the reeds, following the scent but taking a much longer route and thus reducing the possibility of us catching up with our quarry. I decided that we should take the shorter route through the reeds, hoping we might thus catch up by reducing the gap between us. Two steps later and I regretted my hasty decision to ignore my dog. I was up to my neck in brown, smelly and very cold water. As I sunk into the bog Ally was caught by the jerk in his lead, indeed by the 'jerk' on the other end of his lead. He turned round to stare at me and the look of disdain and astonishment on his face was obvious even in the moonlight. I now had to let go of the lead so that I could pull myself out and he just carried on tracking while I extricated myself from my own folly.

Five minutes later I had to chase after him, boots squelching and completely soaked to the skin. Eventually I caught up with him on the edge of the village but it was now obvious that Ally had lost the track and there was no one around in the middle of the night who might have seen any strange sightings.

So, having abandoned our search, together we made our

way slowly back to the vehicle and with the heater on full and the windows wide open to reduce the awful smell in the cab we drove back to my house, where I very quietly let myself in without disturbing the wife, got out of my filthy, wet things and into a fresh uniform so I could complete my shift. I learnt an old lesson that night: always trust your dog.

PC Paul Krauze

It was a lively Friday night and at 2 a.m. I was patrolling around the centre of Swansea in my van with my dog King when I spotted a car, which had been stolen that evening, going in the opposite direction. I did a quick u-turn and saw it turn beside a multi-storey car park up a lane, which I knew went nowhere. When I caught up with it, the driver was long gone. I parked up behind it and with King we started looking for him.

At the end of the lane was a tunnel that led under the railway; on top I saw a figure, who started to run the moment he spotted us. I challenged him to stop and because it was 2 a.m. I felt confident in releasing King to chase after him and detain him.

Both our suspect and King sprinted away out of sight round a corner and I followed as fast as I could. Rounding the corner, to my absolute horror, I discovered that the street was crowded with people. It was a street full of bars and clubs, it was Friday night and it was chucking out time. There must have been at least 200 people, most of who seemed to be diving for cover into taxis or doorways as they spotted King. I could not see my dog or our fugitive anywhere.

I yelled out: "King, come!" Ten seconds later he reappeared from the crowd running directly towards me. But as he got nearer, he suddenly turned down a small side street where he began barking at a man who was trying to conceal himself against a wall. The man already had bite marks on his arm and his jacket was badly ripped where King must have grabbed him earlier before I called him back to my side.

Apparently he had completely ignored everyone in that crowd of late night revellers as he was totally focused on his running quarry. I was very proud of him that evening but would I do it again? No way!

Luck or Misfortune

South Wales Police Force is a vast organisation with massive resources on which it can call for every sort of incident, ranging from a missing pet through to armed robbery, civil disorder or national emergency. In addition its principal resource, the men and women who make up its ranks, are all highly trained, many of them specialising in certain disciplines or in the use of some very sophisticated equipment. As a result criminals, who choose to carry out their nefarious activities in the SWP area, have a high likelihood of detection and identification.

However, despite all these resources, all this sophisticated kit and all this high level of dedication and training by its people sometimes criminals are caught more by luck than through judgement.

PC Mark Randall

All those of us fortunate enough to work in the SWP Dog Section accept that looking after our dogs is a seven-day a week task. Just like any other dog owner, we have to feed, exercise and care for our dogs whether we are on duty or having a day off. Unless we are away on holiday our dogs live with us at home.

It was a lovely summer's day and I had taken my dog Ally for a walk near Pontypridd. We were having great fun as Ally retrieved the tennis balls I threw for him. Not too far away on the edge of the park, I saw a man get out of a van with a bicycle, which he then threw into the bushes. I called Ally to my side and together we trotted over towards the van and I shouted to the man that I was a police officer and wanted to have a chat.

With that he ran back into the van and I could hear him trying to start it. When I got alongside him and opened the driver's door I could see the dashboard fascia had been pulled away and that he was trying to hot-wire it in order to start it. I now assumed it to be stolen and got the man out and arrested him. However I had no handcuffs and no radio to call for help. But I told Ally to lie down and instructed him to watch so our man did not escape.

I then searched the bloke and found a loaded syringe and a spoon with traces of white powder, which I rather assumed was not face powder. I was now faced with the dilemma of what to do with him.

I decided there was no alternative other than to walk our suspect down to the local nick in Pontypridd, which was about ½ mile away. This we did with Ally very much in close attendance and never taking his eye off our prisoner, which was sufficient to keep him very compliant. When we got into the station we went directly into the custody suite, which was deserted, so we continued right through the building to the front desk where the duty operator could call for an officer to assist.

At last I could hand him over and we could get back to our day off. I heard later that our van driver/litter lout was also wanted for burglary and a whole series of robberies. In interview he subsequently admitted all the various offences and asked for eight more to be taken into consideration. It turned out he was something of a one man crime wave that, despite all the Force's best efforts, had managed to carry on regardless evading capture until that unlucky moment when he chose to appear beside Ally and myself. It was just not his day when he decided to pull over in that park.

PC Cliff Piper

My dog Ben just loved water. Not many German Shepherds are that keen on the wet stuff but for Ben it was his greatest joy to be splashing around in any depth of pond, river or stream. We had been helping investigate a domestic burglary at Pontprennau, in east Cardiff, and together we had tracked from the house and into some fields where Ben had lost the scent. We tried in all directions but he could not pick up that track again. So I took off his harness and allowed him to run free to get some exercise before heading back to the van.

Given his freedom he put his nose in the air, looked over to the right and headed off. I recognised the signs; he had sensed water and that was where he was going to cool off. As he disappeared at speed I heard some yelps and some very human cries of pain, suddenly a man sat up out of the grass where he had been lying. Ben had just run right over the man and 40 kg of German Shepherd had caused some pain as he did so. I ran over and arrested him on suspicion of burglary. I then yelled at Ben who came back somewhat reluctantly and soaking wet from his dip in the river. Together we escorted our suspect back to our waiting colleagues who, of course, assumed somewhat naturally that Ben's amazing power of tracking had brought about this successful conclusion to our search. I was not going to disabuse them on that front.

I never did work out why Ben, normally an excellent tracker, had not picked up this man's scent but only I realised just how unlucky that burglar had been. It was just not his day.

I was on patrol with Ben right in the centre of Cardiff when a report came in of a stolen car, which had been abandoned after a chase right up into the Valleys. As I was the only dog team available, and despite my current location, I was tasked to go and look for the thieves, who had taken off on foot into the surrounding mountainside.

My heart sank as I felt certain that, by the time we got there, any chances of a realistic track were very slim. Still we would give it a try. Forty minutes later I found the abandoned car with the local officers, who were waiting to show me in which direction they had seen the occupants disappearing.

With Ben in his harness we set off into the darkness of the Valley's mountainside. Ben had little scent to follow and I felt we were not actually tracking but hoping that Ben might hear or smell something of our fugitives. We had been gone for about 30 minutes and both Ben and I knew there was no track to follow and no signs of those we sought. Before heading back down to the car Ben decided to have a pee and walked up to a small copse of trees and bushes to do so, even though it was in the middle of the night and no-one was likely to be around – old habits die hard.

Half way through his pee he started to growl quite insistently. Immediately six men jumped up from where they were hiding in the bushes just beside me, begging me not to let Ben have a go at them.

I quickly got Ben under control again, he finished what he was doing and we then escorted our prisoners back to the officers waiting by the car. Another brilliant piece of work by this dog team; no need to be too honest about our pure fortune on that night.

Another lucky break came about through traffic police spotting a man driving while talking on his mobile phone. They pulled him over and, while one officer went to talk to the driver, the other did a routine check putting the registration number through the police computer, which responded by indicating that the owner was suspected of being involved in drugs. So they called me up.

I was with them in just a few minutes. The suspect vehicle was essentially a small car that had been converted into a van. I started by putting Cosmo, my yellow Labrador drugs dog, into the driver's seat where he immediately indicated on some brown powder in the passenger's shelf; this later turned out to be, as we thought, heroin.

I then put him into the area behind the front seats where he was showing lots of interest despite there being nothing obvious to see. So I took a closer look and found a small vent through to the rear of the van.

In here we found some parcels, all neatly wrapped in brown paper, which we all rather assumed would be more drugs ready for delivery until we came to the bottom of the pile, where the last parcel was wrapped in clear plastic. It was money. Lots and lots of used notes totalling £67,000, enough to purchase a very expensive car.

The driver was arrested and on the back of this arrest we went to search his home. Although there was no sign of any further drugs we found a couple of top-of-the-range motorbikes, two brand new cars and a pair of jet skis. He lost the lot and his liberty, all brought about because he had not invested wisely in a hands-free system for his mobile phone!

PC Richard Heath

I'm not sure whether this is a story of luck on our part, misfortune on the criminal's part or just his stupidity in not taking any sensible precautions to keep watch.

It was a knock on the door at lunchtime to serve a search warrant on a house in Pentwyn, a suburb in northern Cardiff. I was there, not just to help with the search with my drugs dog Cracker, but also because it was reported that there was a massive bull mastiff in the house. The Dog Section are usually called on to handle potentially aggressive dogs where they might threaten other officers.

Anyway in this case, when the door was opened by a middle-aged man and his wife, the only danger posed by the bull mastiff, which greeted us in the hall, was death by a thousand licks. With the owner's cooperation we secured him in the kitchen and my colleagues and I could start our search for drugs. While they were searching on the ground floor I headed upstairs with Cracker and decided unusually to start on the 2nd floor and work our way downwards.

At the top of the stairs I turned left and opened the door and walked into what turned out to be a bedroom, but more importantly it doubled up as a dispensary because there at the table was a young man with a set of scales, a big bag of white powder and lots of smaller bags neatly tied up and ready no doubt for distribution to his customers. I had no need for the sophisticated, highly trained nose of Cracker to tell me that this was not glucose, sherbet or talcum powder. This was a drug dealer caught red-handed in the act of preparing his 'deals'.

After a rather shocked young man was arrested and taken downstairs Cracker and I continued our search and found lots more 'deals' and a great deal of equipment usually involved in the distribution of drugs as well as a substantial sum of bank notes in a safe. One more blight on our society had been temporarily relocated out of the city.

PC Dai Conway

Traffic officers had been watching out for a vehicle stolen earlier in the day and although they had spotted it a couple of times they had been unable to stop it and had subsequently lost it in the early evening traffic.

It was now quite late in the evening when I heard that they were now pursuing it as it headed toward the lovely and remote area of Caerphilly Mountain. So I immediately headed that way in case I could help. The roads around there are very twisty so I was not surprised to hear that the thieves in their haste had skidded off the road and rolled the car before heading off into the surrounding countryside on foot. The pursuing officers soon lost them in the dark.

It only took 10 minutes before I arrived at the scene of the crashed car with my dog Sam. My colleagues were now able to point out where the occupants were headed and very quickly Sam and I were in pursuit of them over the fields. I know the area quite well and very quickly realised that Sam was tracking in a large circle back towards the vehicles. I was beginning to lose confidence in his pursuit. Oh ye of little faith!

He was right on the money and so about 30 metres short of the crash site we quietly crept up on our two fugitives who were now lying in the undergrowth watching the police officers on the road. They had no idea that a dog was tracking them. Unlucky them!

PC Dickie Wiseman

One evening I was called to the old disused coke works just to the north of the small town of Beddau, located about halfway between Pontypridd and Llantrisant, just a few miles north of the M4 motorway. Two men with a van had been spotted by a late night dog walker and it sounded as if they were probably stealing valuable copper wiring or other precious metal scrap from the site which had been long abandoned.

I found the van without any problem where it had been left on the lane. So my dog Kai started a track from there which inevitably led directly down to the old industrial site, which consisted of some huge derelict buildings and a lot of overgrown waste ground. Much of the boundary fencing was no longer secure as it had become an exciting place for the local youths to explore and, no doubt, get up to no good.

Kai and I spent quite some time searching the site but I was rather wary of taking Kai into some of the buildings because of the broken glass. So after nearly an hour I decided to call it off and head back to our vehicle. This was an opportunity to let Kai off his leash to let him have a run around before getting back into his cage.

As we headed back up the lane Kai suddenly dived off into the bushes and I rather assumed he had spotted a rabbit or perhaps at this time of the night a hedgehog, so followed him into the undergrowth to find out what sort of local wildlife he had discovered. There hiding just 50 yards from their vehicle were two very frightened men, one lying on top of the other, desperately hoping Kai wouldn't bite them. Unlucky for them that I was so indulgent to my dog.

Life Savers

The stereotypical image of police dogs is that of a vicious dog, only vaguely under loose control on a leash, strangling himself in an effort to sink his fangs into anyone within range. As you will have seen, this is far from the truth. Although on command the general-purpose police dog can prove to be quite intimidating to the ne'er-do-well or drunken low-life, they are all highly trained and quite capable of doing their job without any form of aggression unless commanded to be a trifle 'nasty'.

It is also important that they can carry out their search role without culminating in an attack because often they are tasked with finding perfectly innocent people, who have committed no crime and provide no threat to anyone but who just happen to be lost. Very often these people will be very vulnerable for one reason or another. They may be elderly and confused or with learning disorders of one form or another. For these people in South Wales police dogs have often proved to be lifesavers.

PC Richard Heath

It was the foulest of nights in February 2005 when we learnt that an elderly patient in Llwynypia Hospital had left his bed, dressed only in his pyjamas, and wandered off into the adjacent countryside. It could not have been a more disgusting winter's night; it was cold, wet and blowing a gale. Llwynypia is a small ex-mining village halfway up the Rhondda valley; the hospital lies on the eastern side of the valley surrounded by forestry on the steep valley side.

Lots of people had been out looking for the old gentleman ever since he went missing but without any success. That had been some hours before in daylight. Now it was totally dark. The helicopter was grounded by the weather and so when I turned up with my dog Max the outlook did not seem great. Not least because many people – not unnaturally – had been out searching, Max's job was not going to be easy. But as always he was only too eager to start the search; the weather was not a problem for him.

We started our search at the old man's bedside and Max quickly started to track out of the hospital and then down the 200 feet descent of the very steep hillside. I had left him off his leash once we had left the hospital and as I stumbled and fell trying to keep up with him on the treacherous forest slope I could hear him barking which told me that he had found our quarry. It was a huge relief to me and, when I relayed the news, to all the staff and my colleagues waiting above us.

It transpired, and I am not at all surprised, that the patient had fallen for most of that 200 feet and when I got to him he was covered in many cuts and bruises. But nothing was broken and so we managed to get him back into the hospital where he eventually made a full recovery. He was lucky that night because if Max had failed to find him there was no way anyone else would have managed to locate him where he had fallen. He certainly would not have survived the night.

For this incident Max was awarded the PDSA's 'Commendation for Devotion to Duty'. He was only the 19th animal to be honoured with this award since its launch in 2001.

PC Dave Smith

When someone attempts to take their own life overdosing on drugs there is only a very short timeframe in which to get to them. If the drugs do not kill directly then very often, particularly in winter, the environment will do the job even more quickly. Thus time is of the essence in such a situation.

I was called late one evening with my dog Farro to the town of Barry where a man had swallowed a large quantity of prescription drugs and then left his home. Not only were a large number of local police deployed to search the local area but so also was the helicopter with all its sophisticated thermal imaging equipment.

Quite close to the man's house was a large recreation ground which was surrounded by hedges and very dense undergrowth. It was my decision to search this vast area in a clockwise pattern and Farro set off, concentrating on the hedges and the overgrown area beyond as we could see quite clearly if our man was in the well manicured recreation area. We had been searching for 20 minutes, which shows how large an area this was, and we were close to getting back to our start point when Farro started to bark. Underneath the hedge was our quarry, unconscious but still breathing and very much alive.

Within minutes the paramedics had joined us and were treating him in the back of the ambulance. But it had been a close run thing. If I had decided to search in an anti-clockwise pattern we would have found him within five minutes but hindsight is a wonderful thing.

Farro and I were also involved in a rather different type of life-saving incident when we were called to Neath to assist in the search for a missing 12 year old autistic boy.

His father had called the police, not because he thought his son's life was in immediate peril, but rather because he thought he had gone off with two older boys whom he did not trust to look after his vulnerable son. Indeed one of these two was a persistent young offender well known to the local bobbies.

In this case we had no start point from which to track, so we initially set off in the van to patrol the area looking for three kids, probably up to no good. After about 30 minutes I spotted three youths looking into parked vehicles in a street. When they spotted my highly visible police car they legged it into a rear lane. But I spotted where they were hiding and shouted to them to come out or I would release my dog. At this they scarpered down an adjacent alley and I released Farro to locate them. Two went one way and the other another, so Farro pursued the two and disappeared off at great speed out of sight as both the boys and he could far outpace me.

But this was one of our very first operational deployments together and my immediate thought was "Oh no, I've lost my new police dog already"! I followed where I was pretty sure they had gone, across another street and down another lane into a small housing estate. Farro suddenly reappeared through a gap in a fence, almost as if he was looking for me, and indicated quite clearly that he had his quarry in the garden.

So I looked over the fence and could see two youths trying to hide rather unsuccessfully in a small garden. There really was nowhere for them to go so I called Farro back to my side and called for the local bobbies to escort the boys away. One of these two was the lad we were looking for and so he could be safely returned to his dad.

As no offences had been committed there was nothing further for us to do. However I suspect that the young lad would probably remember the fright he had experienced from being chased by a large police dog and would choose whom he went out with rather more carefully in future. Certainly his father was exceedingly grateful to have his vulnerable son returned to him without any harm done to him or by him. It may not have been a 'life-saving' operation like some others but certainly I felt that it had been a very worthwhile 'catch' as, if he had been allowed to continue wandering the streets with these two, the circumstances might have been very different.

PC Mark Frowen

It was way back in 1994 and I was working with my very first and favourite dog Ben when we were tasked to Caerphilly where a stolen car was being driven round the town at speed by a joy-rider having his thrills. Eventually I found the car abandoned on the small rural road leading to the village of Rudry. This suited me down to the ground as we were surrounded by forest and moor and there was little traffic or other people to worry about. So Ben and I set off in pursuit of the driver – which you might think would result in the routine arrest of a suspected criminal but actually this turned into a much more dramatic life-saving operation.

We set off for about one mile along the hard surface of the lane and reached the railway where we went up over a bridge. But suddenly Ben stopped dead in his tracks, paused for a moment as if thinking carefully and weighing the options, then turned back on himself and went down some steps on to the railway.

We continued to track along the railway for about 10 minutes and there in the distance I could see, and hear, our fugitive lying beside the railway track laughing uproariously. He was waving his arms about as if he wanted to attract our attention and be caught. At this stage I decided to play it safe and after the usual warning I released Ben giving him the command to "Hold him", which is essentially telling him to restrain our suspect by biting him. But I could see in the beam of my torch that Ben, having got alongside him, refused to grab his arm, which was very unusual as he was never reluctant to bite whenever possible.

As I got close I saw why. Our suspect was going nowhere; he had been hit by a passing train and was very badly injured indeed, having lost his left leg. His laughter was hysterics as he was in shock, losing blood fast and certainly would not have lasted for long if we had not found him when we did. Even so it took some time for the paramedics to turn up and so I had to provide first aid, if only to stop the incredible loss of blood.

He survived but his joyriding days were over and he had much to be grateful for in Ben's tracking skills.

A rather more conventional life saving task that I carried out, this time with my dog Harry, was in Aberdare where we were sent in mid winter and in the middle of the night to look for a patient missing from a nursing home.

This middle-aged woman suffered from a mental health condition and had decided, despite the freezing temperatures outside, to climb out of a window dressed only in her pyjamas and to go walkabout in the countryside. The weather was awful, so bad that the helicopter was grounded: thus it was just me and Harry who might be able to find her before the wind, the rain and the cold killed her.

We found the window from which she had escaped and headed up the adjacent mountainside on a very positive track. In these awful conditions I was really struggling to keep up with Harry as it seemed that for every three steps I took forward I slid back two. The gorse constantly caught my trousers and jacket and despite my powerful torch the dreadful weather really restricted our visibility. But Harry kept his nose down, was very patient with his much slower Dad, and together we progressed higher and higher up the mountainside.

It must have been 30 minutes of this scrambling before

eventually my torch beam illuminated our quarry, lying under a large gorse bush, conscious – just, but very much in the early stages of hypothermia.

She had survived her ordeal but without Harry's skills she would never have had a chance on the side of the mountain on that dreadful night.

PC Ieuan Evans

This was a rather strange "life-saving" incident which did not involve any tracking at all. I had been called to a flat in Porthcawl early one evening from where a woman had rung the police in hysterics seeking help because her husband was trying to take his life by slashing his wrists with a large kitchen knife, fortunately with not too much success.

When I arrived at the address I decided to take my dog Orla up the stairs with me, not really knowing what to expect when we got into the flat. The wife, who was sobbing hysterically, let us in to what was a very small but self-contained flat and there, in the middle of the kitchen, stood her husband with a large kitchen knife in his right hand. I could see various cuts on his left forearm from where, despite failing to find an artery, blood was dripping everywhere.

He grinned at me rather inanely and I instructed him in a loud voice, with Orla close by my side, to put the knife on the table in front of him. He looked totally blank and did nothing. So I told him again and on the third attempt he seemed to register what I was saying and slowly placed the knife on the table.

My next request was for him to move away so that he could not reach down and grab the knife again. That inane look again covered his face so I moved forward to get him physically to step back from the table but he stood his ground and struggled to get away from my grasp. At least it allowed me to get the wretched knife out of his reach before I instructed Orla to hold him. She immediately grabbed him by the calf of his left leg and in so doing knocked him over and on to the floor where he calmed down at once. Once I felt he was no threat to himself or anyone else, I told her to release him which she did immediately.

So now I could call in the paramedics who had been waiting outside until it was safe for them to come in. Our victim was now looking totally bemused and as he was being led out of the flat to the ambulance he turned to me and Orla and with a big smile said "Thank you both so much for all your help and kindness, I am most grateful".

Even in rather weird circumstances it is nice to be appreciated.

PC Rob Jones

To find a vehicle on the roof of a building is quite strange, even in the middle of a night shift when your weary eyes are beginning to play you up and you are seeing all sorts of strange things in the darkness; but there it was, one of those unexceptional Japanese cars sitting on the top of the old lifeboat shed below the cliff at Mumbles. It was no mystery how it had got there, the broken barriers told their own story from the cliffside road above it. I assumed it had been stolen and the thief had lost control of it, crashed it through the railings and then abandoned it on the roof where it had ended up. So having reported the incident to Control on my radio, I got my dog Zac out of the van, put him in his harness and off we set to look for our driver.

Zac set off up the path towards the top of the cliff. But I could hear voices behind us on the beach and, given that it was the middle of the night and therefore they were unlikely to be topping up their tan, I rather assumed the voices were kids who had crashed the car and were now escaping back towards the town. So I made the mistake of not trusting my dog who I thought was leading me on a wild goose chase entirely in the wrong direction.

But when we got on to the beach we found our driver, who had actually run up the cliff and then jumped off trying to commit suicide. Presumably that was what he was attempting when he drove his car off the cliff road but in the dark had not realised that the lifeboat station was below. The voices were people trying to help him, although what they were doing there at that time of night I never did find out. But it turned out none of them had any idea about first aid so I asked them to disperse, called up the paramedics and then started to try my first aid techniques on our man. That is not easy when you have a large inquisitive police dog alongside, who is determined to help out in any way he can, not least in ensuring that the patient does not come round and attack his Dad.

I cast around for a place for him to lie down where he could feel that he could defend me if he had to but otherwise was well out of my way. Perfect for that was a large raised ledge on the face of the cliff and I got him to lie down up there.

A short while later I was joined by the paramedics who could take over from me rather more effectively. I explained to them what I understood to have happened and one of them shone his torch up the cliff to see how far the drop was from the top. As he did so the beam illuminated Zac's eyes which glared back from the dark and terrified them both until I explained that it was not some wild wolf-like creature which inhabited the cliffs at Mumbles at night, just Zac, my German Shepherd, watching what was going on.

PC Carl John

A different sort of life was saved when I was called out to the M4 around lunchtime on a busy Monday by the motorway traffic cops, who had spotted a dog dodging the traffic and so panicked he would not allow anyone near him.

Normally for catching dogs we have some quite sophisticated equipment, including poles and nets, that make the job easier but they are more suitable for catching dogs that attack you rather than run away so we had nothing suitable for this particular case. Traffic units had put a slow block on the motorway, not just for the safety of the dog but, very sensibly, for the safety of the road users who might only too easily cause an accident while trying to avoid the Mutt. Anyway having found the dog and assessed the situation I decided that the old fashioned way was best.

I got out of the vehicle and tried to entice it to me with various treats that I always carry in my pockets. I could see he was curious and his natural greed was beginning to overcome his fear and panic. But having got to within 10 yards of me to pick up a treat, which I had thrown on the ground, he would come no closer. Still 10 yards was close enough for me; I sprinted out and, as he turned to run away, I launched myself in a huge rugby tackle, worthy of the Swansea Ospreys, and caught him. Having got hold of him there was no way I was going to let go of him again.

The traffic could flow safely once more while I took the dog to a local RSPCA centre where they scanned him, found a microchip and thus I could return him to one very relieved owner who lived just a short distance away.

To put this story into further context, PC Carl John used to play centre in Rugby Union, the dog was a Bichon Frise and, having been caught, it bit him! Also it had already managed to side step a

Traffic Officer in a move worthy of Gareth Edwards, which had left the officer on his backside down a steep grass bank.

PC Sam Dunstan

We had already had a busy Saturday night in Cardiff, sorting out a large fight at a wedding party, when my dog Yatz and I were tasked to help look for a man with mental health issues who was armed with a knife and was threatening to use it on himself. Apparently he was clinically depressed and a serious danger to himself and to anyone who got in his way. All we knew of his whereabouts was that he was somewhere in northern Cardiff, which was not really very helpful! Certainly there was nowhere from which we could track as we had no idea from where he had gone missing.

So I began to search on foot all the local parks where Yatz might just pick up something untoward in the undergrowth. As it was the middle of a Saturday night in August I was not sure who or what else we might find! We had been going from park to park for about an hour and we were starting out on another one when I heard on the radio that the man had phoned his sister and had told her he was near an Astroturf pitch. I looked down, I was standing on Astroturf, the only Astroturf pitch I knew of in this area. Perhaps our luck was in and we might yet get our man before any harm was done. Besides I was dying for a cup of tea!

I shouted a challenge and sent Yatz to search. Yatz covered every inch of the Astroturf and surrounding area but found nothing. I was now getting a bit fed up at being given the run around by this person, who had again rung his sister saying he was somewhere else. I decided to call it a day and head back towards the van. I called Yatz to me and put him on the lead. As we walked, Yatz started to pull on the lead and tried to take me back in the direction we had come. Having learnt my lesson by not trusting the dog once before, I let him pull me towards a community centre building which was a short distance away from the Astroturf, across a lane. At the back of the community centre was a patch of waste ground overgrown with long grass and weeds. I was convinced that Yatz was messing me around so I gave him the command "Where is he?" just to let him get it out of his system and let him off his lead.

Yatz ran directly onto the waste ground into the undergrowth and started to bark. Even then I thought perhaps he had found a rabbit or hedgehog; I ran over to him to see what he had found. When I got to him, all I could see was his tail wagging inside the long grass. As I moved the grass to get a better look, a man jumped up from where he was hiding and was very agitated and aggressive. Yatz, seeing this as a threat to his Mum instantly defended me by angrily snarling and fiercely staring at him daring him to come nearer to me.

I quickly put Yatz under control and calmed the bloke down. Our man was clearly quite a vulnerable person and needed some medical assessment. As we waited for the paramedics to collect him with an ambulance, I can remember thinking to myself, what a night! First all the excitement of the wedding party fight, then your dog goes and bites a vulnerable missing person with mental health issues. I then got a grip of myself and did a reality check and realized that Yatz had done his job yet again and he had probably saved a life. I should be thankful for such a talented dog.

PC John Johnson

I was sent, with my dog Millie, to a house in Neath where a man had made some serious threats to hurt his girlfriend. She had managed to escape and reported to the police that he had a handgun. The house consisted of two flats and he was in the first floor one. All the neighbours had been evacuated and, by the time I got there, it was really a siege situation.

One of the armed response unit officers, who was watching the property very closely through his weapon sights, reported that he could see smoke through the window of the front room. Shortly afterwards we heard a shot. The decision was made to go in with myself and Millie supporting the firearms officers.

We forced open the front door leading to the staircase which had been barricaded with various bits of furniture, a TV, a fridge and a freezer. Pouring down the stairs was thick, black, acrid smoke but I managed to lift Millie over the fridge and sent her up the stairs to locate and detain our suspect. I lost sight of her within a couple of steps but then suddenly the smoke cleared and I could see our man collapsed from the smoke at the top of the stairs with Millie standing over him, barking furiously. I called her back straightaway, helping her once again to negotiate the various bits of furniture blocking the stairs.

I then passed her back to officers waiting outside before, having quickly cleared a passage up the stairs, myself and two of my colleagues forced our way up to the top of the stairs to the casualty and dragged him down out into the fresh air. He was sent off to hospital under escort and was subsequently charged successfully.

PC John Johnson received a Chief Constable's Certificate of Commendation for Bravery for this incident.

A Good Night Out

Both Cardiff and Swansea city centres on a Friday or Saturday night are usually humming. The two cities gather in people of all ages and from all backgrounds from a wide area, all determined on having a 'Good Night Out'. For some a 'Good Night Out' is a visit to one of many excellent restaurants of South Wales to enjoy a good meal with fine wine in the company of friends, for others it is meeting with some mates for a few convivial beers but for some a 'Good Night Out' can be rather different.

PC Jones Roberts

One particular Saturday in the summer of 2011 I was patrolling in the Swansea city centre area with my 'Ella' when I heard on the radio that the control room was receiving various reports of large numbers of two well known families drinking at certain watering holes and that to ensure an evening to remember they intended this to culminate in a fight later in the night. Each to their own it would seem when considering what constitutes a 'Good Night Out' but public brawling is against the law, it endangers others and, not least, for most people it rather detracts from their own enjoyable evening in Swansea. However, knowledge of a forthcoming fight is all very well, stopping it happen is another matter entirely. All Ella and I could do was maintain a presence in the area to provide reassurance for the law-abiding public and deterrence to the potential pugilists.

It was shortly after midnight when I was stopped by a woman who told me that two families were about to face up for a fight in Princess Way, right in the heart of the city, as part of their long term family feud. Some of these families have been feuding for so long that they have probably forgotten the original cause of their mutual animosity. But family 'honour' is very important to them and being seen not to fight once having been 'called out' would be a big blemish on the family name and therefore the fight was inevitable.

Having parked the van at the end of the road I approached Princess Way on my own but soon realised that this was obviously the planned venue for a massive bust up involving a lot of people. In the middle were the fighting men surrounded by a large number of supporters, no doubt from their respective families. Meanwhile there were plenty of ordinary folk coming out of the pubs and clubs trying to go home.

Just as I arrived the fighting started so, having radioed for support, I returned to the van to bring out Ella. Immediately she summed up what was happening and started to bark vociferously. Although this provided a certain diversion, particularly amongst the support teams, the fighting continued. I shouted out the usual warnings, albeit it was somewhat difficult to make myself heard over the sounds of the women screaming their vitriol at each other and over the noise of Ella's enthusiastic barking, and released 30 kilos of dog to sort out the fight.

She headed straight into the thick of the action and took hold of the main protagonist. The fight broke up immediately as the man tried to defend himself from one large biting machine. At the same time I could hear the sirens of my own support team getting closer and closer. The various people who had been taking such an active and noisy part in goading on the fight somehow, on hearing the sirens, seemed to melt away, blending quietly in amongst the innocent public and leaving me with two men immobilised by their fear of Ella and her bite. She just stood over them looking fierce. They knew if either moved they would get bitten again.

The result of the evening was two men arrested and, apart from them, no-one was hurt. Princess Way once again was safe to travel on and very few people, apart from these two families, had had their 'Good Night Out' ruined.

PC Gareth Roberts

For some people there is nothing to beat a good car chase for a 'Good Night Out'. Thrills and spills in fast motor cars are regular entertainment for most of us but generally the entertainment takes place in a cinema, in front of a TV or a computer game. Sadly there is a small element of society who likes to experience it for real but always, of course, in someone else's car and at a huge risk to the general public.

It was 2 a.m. in early January when I heard about a joy-rider being pursued by police in Merthyr Tydfil. He had stolen a very fast car and was having the time of his life behind the wheel. He knew he would shake off his police pursuers if he did something really stupid like drive the wrong way down a dual carriageway; which is exactly what he did when he hit the A470. Thank goodness it was 2 a.m. and the road was just about deserted apart from the odd lumbering lorry.

Although the officers had lost him when they decided to stop the pursuit, it was not long before they found the car, all in one piece and parked up in the Gellideg estate on the west side of town. But of the young driver, there was no sign.

I started the search by deploying my dog Gabe into an area of woodland that lies between this large council estate and the A470 dual carriageway. But Gabe gave no indication of having any scent to follow either in the wood or on the estate roads. So I came back to the local divisional officers and suggested that they and their vehicles withdraw from the area and Gabe and I would stay around to see if the driver showed up again.

So we found a nice dark area in which to hide and we did not have to wait very long. Twenty minutes later I saw a youth, matching the description I had been given, leaving the estate on foot and heading into town. At that hour of the morning there was not exactly a whole crowd of people with which to mingle.

I only had to shout my challenge once and he stood very still indeed. Gabe was barking enough to wake the entire estate. When he heard the dog he had no intention of reliving the thrills of his chase from earlier in the night. I whistled up my divisional colleagues who were waiting a short distance away and the youth was arrested and taken away into custody. He had had his 'Good Night Out', now came the retribution!

Dogs are Fallible

The South Wales Police Force runs one of the most highly respected dog training units in the country. Dozens of dogs from regions all over Wales and the south west of England, as well as from all corners of the UK from Norfolk to Cheshire to the Police Service of Northern Ireland, are trained at Bridgend every year as well as occasional dogs from overseas. To be accepted on operations they have to pass some very rigorous tests and many fail. However, no matter how rigorous the training and how harsh the assessment on operations there may be certain occasions for which there is nothing in the syllabus. As a result police dogs can be fallible.

PC Carl John

It was after midnight in mid summer when the call came for me to investigate an alarm activated in a cricket club pavilion in Swansea. There was very little traffic on the roads and with the blue light flashing it only took five minutes to get there. The first thing I noticed was that the front door had been forced. Given the short space of time since the activation there was a strong chance of the burglar still being inside. I thought how satisfying that would be – to actually catch the burglar on the job.

Having issued a challenge from the doorway I let my new dog, Dylan, off his leash and instructed him to search inside. Within a minute Dylan was barking furiously which told me that he had found the intruder. I turned on my torch and entered the building and very quickly caught up with Dylan, all the while planning to make an arrest of someone caught in the premises and bask in all the glory of a red-handed arrest.

In the bar Dylan had indeed found a man, about 6 feet tall and quite well dressed with a pint of foaming bitter in his hand. The man, very sensibly given the aggressive dog inches away from him, was standing very still but it was not Dylan's furious barking which had kept him in this position. The 'suspect' was a full size cardboard cut-out advertising the many fine qualities of the product from the Worthington Brewery.

PC Mark Frowen

Sam was my black Labrador trained to search specifically for drugs. Sam's greatest love in training, like most police dogs, was his tennis ball with which he was always rewarded for every success in finding his quarry. As with most search dogs he became obsessed with tennis balls, as he knew that this was the sign that he had done well and that his Dad was very pleased with him.

On one particular search we had been sent to check out the house of a suspected drug dealer, a seemingly wealthy man who lived very comfortably in a relatively new house in Penarth.

The technical search team, without a dog to help them, had been through various downstairs rooms, with no hint of drugs anywhere, and eventually they had made their way into the kitchen. Like the rest of the house the kitchen was very well equipped and obviously only recently fitted out with stylish and expensive units. Sam started to cast about with his usual enthusiasm and after only 30 seconds started to indicate very strongly at the cupboards in one corner. I immediately emptied out all the contents – pots, pans and casserole dishes – on to the floor but after five minutes still had not found anything significant. Sam meanwhile continued to indicate.

Having worked with Sam for some years, I had come to trust his judgement implicitly and so I felt that we were almost certainly onto something really significant. I unscrewed the cupboard units and now Sam was indicating at the kickboards at the back. Totally convinced now that we were on to something substantial I enlisted the help of my colleagues and together we continued to dismantle the cupboards either side until we could access the kickboards at the rear. This lovely newly built kitchen was now really looking a total mess. Most of the contents of the cupboards were scattered over the floor and the kitchen units were in bits.

Eventually we managed to rip the boards off the wall and there we made the big discovery – a rather old tennis ball. We left, not in a cloud of glory, and Sam did not get to keep the ball.

PC Derek Francis

It was a visit by the Prime Minister, who was then Margaret Thatcher, to the Fairwater Conservative Club in Cardiff that led to an explosive search task for me and my Labrador, Toby. No doubt like many Prime Ministerial visits, this one had only been announced at the last minute, so it was all rather chaotic when we and the rest of the team descended on the building. The catering staff were still laying the tables for dinner, others were putting out chairs around the hall and yet more people from Conservative Central Office were laying out all the displays and marketing material on the stage which would be the backdrop for the PM's appearance on TV that night.

As a temporary measure the caterers had put the cheese platters on each of the chairs on the stage prior to moving them on to the tables. Like most dogs Toby always regarded cheese as one of his favourite treats and he very quickly made the appreciation that lined up on the stage were rows of his

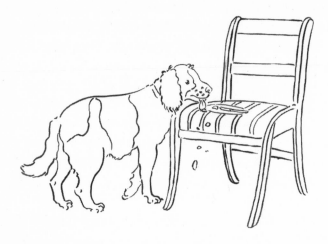

favourite snack. Before anyone could do anything about it he had jumped up on to the stage and worked his way rapidly along the line of chairs, taking a chunk off each platter.

Fortunately no-one, apart from me and one colleague, had spotted this indiscretion; everyone was far too busy. Pretending just to follow him up on his searching I very swiftly, but quite nonchalantly, made my way on to the stage, extracting my ever present Swiss Army penknife with which I cut out the evidence from each dish, all the time pretending to be inspecting the stage and the chairs for hidden devices.

No-one ever noticed! No-one, until they read this story, was ever the wiser.

PC Ian Hemburrow

As part of their induction training as a dog handler, probationers are occasionally attached to working dog teams on operational patrols so that they can appreciate the value of the dogs and see how they work. I had volunteered to have one such probationer attached to me for a night shift; it is always nice to have some company on a quiet night and we had had a number of those recently. But that evening we were called to a burglary in Pyle Industrial Estate, near Porthcawl.

I was working with a white German Shepherd called Charlie at the time. A lovely dog with very striking looks. On arriving at the scene of the burglary, I put Charlie on his leash and we began tracking with the probationer running along behind. We jogged determinedly down the busy road, crossed over a roundabout and into a dense wooded area.

Now that we were clear of traffic I released Charlie from his harness and he went flying off in pursuit of his quarry. After just half a minute he started to bark loudly and so I could turn to the probationer and say with total confidence, and not a little pride, "Got him!" As we followed the sound of the barking, I extracted my handcuffs ready to make an arrest, fully expecting to find a terrified suspect cowering on the ground.

Eventually we caught up with Charlie who was still barking with considerable menace. In the light of my torch we found the source of his undivided attention – a hedgehog, tightly rolled into a ball and not planning to unroll until this frightening and noisy creature had gone away.

PC Glan Osbourne

Dogs and handlers may well spend many hours of the day in their vehicle. I generally kept the door between the dog cage and the front cab area open so that my dogs had closer contact with me, which is nice for us all, and also so that I could extract either quickly if required to deploy in a hurry.

It had been one of those days with not a great deal happening when I was tasked to a house in Cimla where there had been a report of some suspicious character behaving strangely. Being a suburb on the eastern side of Neath, Cimla is one of those mining communities built on the side of the valley wherever there was any possibility of finding space for development. I parked up on the very steep residential street overlooking the town and went into the house to get more details from the lady who had phoned in the report.

I was in there for about 10 minutes, not even long enough for a cup of tea, and when I came out, of the vehicle there was no sign. My initial thought was that someone had stolen it, with my dogs inside, which on reflection was really fairly unlikely as my German Shepherd, Sam, would have made mincemeat of anyone other than me entering the driver's door.

I walked out further into the street and there it was, 200 metres away at the bottom end of the road where fortunately it had collided with another stationary car, which had halted its progress further down the hill. Although both my vehicle and the parked car were badly damaged the dogs were fine if somewhat shaken. But Sam was now sitting in the front cab, looking rather sheepish (if that is possible in a German Shepherd!), as he had obviously managed to knock off the handbrake. I never left him alone with access to the cab again. It made for an interesting insurance claim form.

PC Dai Conway

Some people have some very strange things in their homes. Late one evening I responded to an alarm call in a large manor house deep in the countryside near the town of Nelson. I quickly found the reason for the alarm sounding; there was a back door ajar. There were no signs of any forced entry but, as the house was completely dark and the alarm was making enough noise to waken the entire countryside, let alone anyone inside, I decided to let my dog, Sam, go in to have a search around.

I made the customary warning by the open door, trying to make myself heard over the sound of the alarm, and then let

Sam off his leash, following along close behind. The door led into a long corridor and at the end of it suddenly an old man with bleach-blond, white hair, looking rather like Einstein on a bad hair day, and dressed all in Victorian clothes, loomed up out of the dark and announced clearly and loudly "Fair thee well!"

Sam immediately launched himself at this apparition but there was nothing to grab hold of. In the dark this had both of us terrified and I turned and fled, calling for Sam to follow me; he needed no repeat command. Once outside we both calmed down and took stock. Eventually I decided that there was nothing for it but to go back inside if I was to be able to confirm that there were no burglars around. Not least it would not look good in my report if I made claims that a ghost had stopped us going any further. So I put Sam at the 'sit' position by the door while I went back in with my most powerful torch to investigate.

As I crept forward I found the light switch, which helped to calm me down not a little and when I reached the same spot at the end of the corridor exactly the same thing happened. However with all the lights on it was now apparent that the Einstein look alike was in fact just a hologram.

What a great way of ensuring any intruder went no further into the house.

PC Walter Pennell

Every so often there are training sessions for the various search dogs and their handlers, so that both of them are constantly kept up to date with the latest developments from the criminal world and are also regularly assessed by other handlers or instructors.

I had taken my drugs search dog, Jess, on one such training day at the Grand Pavilion, situated on the Esplanade at

Porthcawl; a vast building with plenty of scope for hiding things in unusual places. This particular training location was considered a 'live venue' as the Pavilion staff continued to do their normal work while the teams did their search exercises. Thus the dogs were faced with a realistic working environment, lots of day to day smells everywhere and the odd temptation which might distract them.

Jess had been working successfully for some 10 minutes and had already made some impressive finds of drugs planted around the building by my instructor. We moved into the main reception area where one young lady was sitting behind the desk ready to greet any visitors coming in through the main door. Suddenly Jess indicated to me that she was on to another 'find' in a bag behind the desk. But the instructor who had planted each one of the caches around the building declared that he hadn't hidden anything in this area.

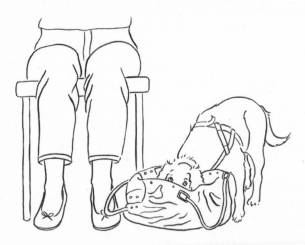

At that point Jess came out from behind the desk with a large sandwich in her mouth and ran off down a corridor, just like a naughty child, so she could eat it without any hassle from her Dad. I meanwhile had to go out and buy some new sandwiches for the receptionist's lunch. It took me many months of ribbing from my mates before that particular incident was erased from the records.

PC Paul Krauze

I had a wonderful drugs dog called Dylan, but he was a very timid Sprocker (Springer/Cocker Spaniel cross) who rarely ventured far from my side. One day I was walking him, while off-duty, around some of the local fields near my home when I realised he was no longer with me.

I knew he had not run ahead so I turned and retraced my steps back the way we had come, back through a gate and into the previous field. The light was beginning to fade so I thought my eyes were playing tricks on me when I saw what I thought was a dead sheep actually moving. As I got closer I suddenly spotted that it had a strange black and white tail that was wagging ten to the dozen. Dylan was actually inside the sheep and was enjoying a feast.

I eventually managed to get him out but he was not a pretty sight. Quite the smelliest, most disgusting dog I had ever seen. The sheep had been dead for well over a week and should have been removed a long time ago. It was crawling with maggots and buzzing with flies. Now they were all buzzing around my dog that was covered in blood and guts. But he was a very happy dog until I got him home where we spent over an hour scrubbing him from head to tail.

He may have been a very good drugs dog but he was also a very greedy one. During his life he had to have five operations to remove items that he had swallowed.

PC Steve Atkinson

In the early hours of darkness one wet summer's evening, I and my dog Dave were tasked with another colleague,

PC Geraint Bruford and his dog Ronnie, to assist officers in the Ely area of Cardiff at a house where a burglary had just taken place. Two men had been disturbed by the owner of the house who had chased them into some nearby fields where they had disappeared into the darkness.

We all set off in hot pursuit across the fields tracking a path, which led to where a large pipe crossed the River Ely, which was in full flood. I decided that, as the river was flowing at such a rate, we would not risk crossing the pipe although in my torch beam I could see the two men attempting to hide on the other side. Having realised they had been spotted the two suspects made off into the nearby woods. So I got on my radio and the local police unit, who were still on the road, crossed the river by the road bridge and approached the woods.

Once we saw the others had arrived there, we and our dogs made our way back to our vehicles and then drove round to join them at the woods in case we could provide any further help. When we got there we decided that Geraint would send in Ronnie to track them down, holding back Dave in reserve. Ronnie went into the woods on his own while we stood on the edge for quite some while. After a few minutes, Geraint called him back before sending him out again. Once more we waited to hear the tell-tale sounds of discovery but there was just a very loud silence. We knew the two men were in there and that they could not have gone in very far. Eventually Ronnie returned to Geraint who suggested that it was Dave's turn to go and look.

So I released Dave from his harness and he flew off with his usual enthusiasm, no doubt tempered by the idea of showing up Ronnie (or was the competitive spirit entirely in my mind?). Less than 30 seconds later we heard the sounds of barking and the usual whimpering from a human who had just been bitten on the arm. Geraint and I quickly followed up the sounds and found the two men terrified and only too happy to have been caught.

But it was still a mystery as to why Ronnie had not found them during his search as they were not very far in from the edge of the woods and he was a particularly well-trained dog. So having arrested the two fugitives I asked them how they had concealed themselves from the first dog. They admitted that Ronnie had actually found them but one of them, who owned a German Shepherd himself, had stood his ground with confidence and told the dog to sit, which he did. He had eventually been called back by his handler and then sent back out again. It having worked the first time, they pulled the same trick again with apparent success, until once again Ronnie was called back in by Geraint.

On the third attempt, with Dave, they had no idea it was a different dog so were horrified when he launched himself at them and their words of command had no effect. For them it was not third time lucky.

Sadly for them, not all dogs are equally fallible.

Plans Change

The best laid plans of mice and men often go awry. Or as Robbie Burns put it in his native Scots language:

The best laid schemes o' mice an' men
Gang aft agley

This succinctly summarises the anecdotes in this chapter when events crowd in on planned operations, things just go wrong or the operation turns out successful despite the 'plan' being somewhat inadequate to the situation.

Fortunately police officers seem to have a default setting that things are not going to work as planned and therefore they can adapt rapidly whatever the circumstances. Of course, also, things may not actually be as they seem.

PC Sam Dunstan

One Saturday night in August, my dog Yatz and I were on patrol in Cardiff when a call came over the radio reporting a large fight in the Llandaff area. Llandaff is usually one of the quieter areas of the city with very little in the way of public disorder going on, so the call came as a surprise.

We made our way across the city and arrived at the pub just in time to see uniformed officers chasing four men along the road nearby, away from a large crowd that had gathered outside the pub. I quickly drove the van towards them and saw that the officers had detained three of them in the grounds of the nearby school. I got out of the van and spoke to one of the officers who explained that one of the men had been lost in the school grounds.

I quickly ran to the van and opened up the back. I deployed Yatz, grabbed hold of his collar and ran into the school grounds. Picking up on my adrenaline, Yatz started bouncing along on his back legs like a kangaroo. This is always something he does when he is really excited. I shouted out a challenge, "Police with a dog. Come out now or I will send the dog!" The sound of my voice shouting sent Yatz into a frenzy and he started to shout himself, sounding like some sort of demented werewolf.

No one came out of hiding so I let go of his collar. I have often thought what it must be like for the criminals, as they sit or lie in their hastily found hiding places, listening to the dog panting, getting closer and closer. Like a bizarre game of hide and seek with a sometimes painful ending. It must be terrifying!

Yatz went off like a rocket, sprinting around the school grounds searching. The dog periodically put his nose to the ground to confirm he was going the right way. Then he went into a tennis court on the school grounds, surrounded by a 15-foot high chain link fence. Yatz let out one bark, spun on his hocks, turned and came out of the tennis court, frantically running back the way he had come. I looked at him wondering what the hell he was doing. With that, he pushed his way into the bushes outside the tennis court but directly the other side of where he had first barked. I could then hear a tremulous voice cry out, "Don't let him bite me", followed by a volley of barks.

I ran over to the bushes and saw that Yatz had located our fugitive's hiding place. He was one of the men, about 17 years old and was wearing a shirt, trousers and just his socks. As I approached there was a strong smell of faeces. At first I thought that Yatz might have broken wind with all the excitement of it all but all was to be revealed. I was over the moon believing that we had bagged the bad guy, the one responsible for an assault at the wedding party, but all that quickly changed a short time later. The four men were arrested and taken into custody and further enquiries were made at the pub.

As it turned out, the men we had arrested were the victims of a large fight at a wedding party; they had run because they were in fear for their lives. The poor boy that the dog had found had been beaten up and had lost his shoes in the fracas. Then the poor bloke, being petrified of dogs, had actually curled up into a ball and been frozen in terror when Yatz had found him in the bushes!

Things had not been as they seemed and, although we had prevented anyone getting hurt more seriously, our actions had somewhat scary results for one of the victims of the incident.

PC Dai Conway

There had been a break-in in the middle of the night at a social club in the Rhondda. I had sped up there and when I with my dog Sam met divisional officers with the keyholder at the front door we were not at all sure whether there might be someone still in the club. The entrance was through a large revolving door that opened into a main foyer. Sam and I led off just in case there was someone waiting for us on the other side. I had only taken a couple of steps through the door when Sam started to growl loudly. We all stopped at once and I turned to my colleagues and shouted back to them through the revolving door: "I am pretty sure there is someone here." Two more steps and Sam started to bark loudly. "There is definitely someone in here" I shouted back before shouting my usual warning prior to releasing Sam off his lead to search and detain.

By now his barking was constant and I gave him his command "Go and hold". However, although I had released him he stayed right beside me and refused to move. This was very strange as he was always so keen. I turned my torch beam on to him and suddenly all was made clear. The poor dog was not barking at any burglar, he was barking because his tail was caught in the revolving door and he could not move.

Needless to say the divisional officers thought it hilarious and the story soon spread round the Force, getting better on each telling of the tale of the tail.

PC Rob Jones

I was sent to investigate a report of a disturbance in a house in the little town of Penllergaer, just next to the M4 Services of Swansea East. It sounded like a 'domestic' that had got out of hand. As I pulled up outside the address I had been given, a man, who must have heard the siren and spotted my blue light, left the house at great speed.

A few seconds later I had got my dog, Larrs, out of his cage and, having shouted at the man to stop, without any success, we were soon in hot pursuit. Our fugitive disappeared through the adjoining gardens and we were very close behind. The fences between the gardens on this estate were all relatively low and so we chased him through various gardens, over many fences and through hedges before he went down a path to the side of a house. At the end of this path he vaulted some wooden pallets into another garden rather larger than most. Larrs followed him with ease; I found the pallets more of a challenge because of all the kit I have to wear or carry but eventually struggled over them.

On the other side was a fishpond. I could see Larrs was by now on the other side so rather assumed he had gone through it and it was therefore only inches deep. How wrong can you be? I found myself instantly submerged in cold, muddy water up to my chest. In addition there must have been a deep layer of weed and other vegetable growth on the surface because I really was revolting.

But, having hauled myself out, I did not have time to worry about my appearance; I could hear Larrs barking at the far end of the garden, which told me he had our man. Fortunately my torch was still working fine and in the beam I could see Larrs's tail wagging furiously with his head deep in a thick bush.

I went forward and arrested our suspect before searching him. On his person we found a whole stash of powder which turned out to be heroin and rather more cash, £1,300, than he could account for. He also turned out to be in breach of his bail conditions. All well worth a good smelly soaking.

PC Martin Philips

It was late on a Saturday night when we heard about an alarm sounding at a brewery in Swansea and I went to investigate with my dog Jake. When we arrived the front door was wide open so, with Jake leading but on a leash, we went in. It was pitch dark and I was pondering which way to go when a man jumped out of the darkness right in front of me. I jumped a mile in the air out of shock but Jake reckoned that his Dad was being attacked and launched himself forward, grabbing the man very firmly by the arm.

The man stank of alcohol and when I eventually recovered my composure I shouted at him to lie down on the floor, which he did with alacrity, and Jake released him but continued to keep a very close eye on him to ensure he stayed there.

At this stage our 'assailant' introduced himself as the keyholder who happened to live close by, had heard the alarm and, despite having imbibed an excessive amount of his own product, had come to investigate. He it was who had opened the front door and we soon established there was no break-in; it was a false alarm.

Unfortunately Jake had caused some very nasty wounds

to his arm but, perhaps it was the drink talking, he found the situation all rather funny. We got him off to the hospital to have his wounds tended to and he never made any complaint.

PC Steven Sutton

The Welsh Millennium Centre is a vast public building in the Cardiff Bay area of the city. Back of house is a maze of corridors leading off in every direction. Two of us with our explosive search dogs had been sent there to search the building prior to a visit by the Queen, who was coming to open it officially.

So we set off trying to ensure we covered every part of the building – every room, corridor and other space – in a methodical fashion so nothing was missed out. Once we had completed our search of an area we would close the door behind us before proceeding onwards.

Eventually we reckoned that each room on each floor had been covered and we had nowhere further to search. So we turned to go back to our start point at the entrance. But what we had not realised, with our oh so clever and methodical plan, was that each door locked itself as we closed it and we could not reopen any of them. In addition, although we knew at which end of the building we were, when we eventually contacted the officers at the central reception area we could not identify exactly where in the building we were.

It took 45 minutes for them to find us. I hope the Queen did not get lost later in the day.

PC Steve Atkinson

It was in the middle of the night when we received a call that a burglary was in progress in the St Mellons area of Cardiff. The caller was actually watching three men break into his neighbour's house. So it was that I sped over there with my dog Rocky and arrived there about the same time as officers from the CID. They had spotted a Ford Cortina (this was in 1992!) parked in the lane in which they were confident was the getaway car for the burglars. So they were probably still around, if not actually in the house.

It was at this point that I spotted three men jump out from the bushes further down the lane; one threw down a petrol can while another dropped a pick axe handle before sprinting off down the lane. I shouted out my usual challenge, trying to encourage them not to bother wasting their energy or risking being bitten by my dog which would inevitably catch them – or words to that effect, but they chose to ignore me and kept running.

So I released Rocky, who was raring to go, and he sped off after them. I jogged along behind him. Rounding a corner I found Rocky having something of a one-sided wrestling match with one of our suspects. When I got close I called Rocky off and once he had been released the stupid man decided to have a go at me as I stepped in to handcuff him.

Rocky was not having his Dad attacked by this reprobate and really went for him, biting him vigorously. However, in his enthusiasm to get retribution for the attack on me, he muddled up the two of our anatomies and thus I received a fairly substantial bite on my bum. At this moment reinforcements arrived in the form of the CID officers who helped me detain our rather aggressive suspect.

Rocky and I then took off down the lane once more to bring in the other two. We had not gone very far before Rocky dived into the hedgerow and, not taking any chances this time, took hold of the man who was hiding there. This man however was rather more sensible and, having called Rocky off, I could detain him easily.

Although I had sustained a rather undignified wound in a sensitive area we had caught two of the three burglars. I was pretty certain that the third man would be identified and arrested later.

It was Rocky who was with me when we joined in the pursuit of a stolen Austin Montego (why would you want to steal one of those?!), taken from the Culverhouse Cross car park in western Cardiff. There were five youths on board and we pursued it at speed right across the city and eventually ended up in the Pentwyn area. I was right behind it when the driver lost control, crashed into a wall and the five occupants all took off on foot in different directions.

The front seat passenger was caught by another officer while I set off with Rocky in pursuit of the driver over an adjacent field. What I did not know was that another officer had parked up on the other side of the field and the fugitive ran straight into his arms and began to struggle with him to get released.

Out of the dark came Rocky in full pursuit mode only to spot his quarry struggling on the floor. Sadly Rocky cannot tell the difference between a suspect and a police officer and so, in the fracas, the latter got bitten on both arms. Luckily he had only sustained light grazes, but we had got our thief.

PC Mark Frowen

My explosive search dog, Skye, and I were tasked with other teams to the Pierhead building in Cardiff Bay where we were to clear it for explosives prior to a visit by the Prime Minister. Along with the others we had cleared the ground floor and then the first and the second floors before heading up to the third floor. We had worked our way down a corridor clearing rooms as we went. Then I saw a door that was closed so I opened it. As I did so Skye jumped over my shoulder and through the door. This was one of our party tricks, jumping over my shoulder as I opened doors. Unfortunately this door led directly into the dumb waiter, the lift system used by the catering department to send food up from the kitchens in the basement. Even more unfortunately the lift itself was actually down four floors below us in the basement.

All I could hear was smashing glass at the bottom. I shot off downstairs but had to wait for what seemed like forever before we could find the holder of the key to the basement. But when we eventually got in there and I opened the door to the dumb waiter out jumped Skye. Miraculously he was virtually unharmed with no real injury other than he had a very small cut on his leg. He just shook himself as if nothing had happened and carried on searching.

PC Gareth Roberts

I was tasked to a house up the Cynon Valley, above Aberdare, to support some officers who were having difficulty breaking up what appeared to be a domestic dispute. As happens so often, the moment the officers had tried to intervene they had become the subject of the violence.

As I, with my dog Gabe, went through the front gate I could hear shouting and screaming from inside the house; once inside I discovered a man in the kitchen throwing china mugs at the two divisional officers. He then leant towards the cooker and was about to pick up the chip pan full of fat, so I yelled at the officers to get out of the way and released Gabe to hold and detain our angry man before he could throw that chip pan at any of us. Gabe launched himself at the man's leg to knock him over but I could tell he was not entirely comfortable with this as he ripped off the man's jeans. As the material came away in Gabe's mouth we all looked in astonishment, as the leg was entirely false. No wonder Gabe was rather put out. But this only made him pause momentarily as he renewed his attack, this time to the right arm, and brought the man down on to the floor where the three of us could safely detain him.

False legs were not part of Gabe's training but he coped well nevertheless.

PC Geraint Bruford

It was quite early in the evening when I, accompanied by my dog Ronnie, was tasked to a large department store in the centre of Cardiff to investigate the report of an intruder. Apparently the report of the intruder came from a security guard monitoring the internal cameras, which had shown a man climbing the stairs towards the bedding department on the second floor.

We met two of the local officers and the keyholder at the entrance and he let us in having explained that all the staff had long since gone home and, apart from the window displays, everything was in darkness. As a parting comment, just as we were setting off into the darkness, he told us: "By the way, you do know that the store is haunted, don't you?"

"So," I asked him, "how do you know it wasn't a ghost that you saw on the camera then?"

"Well," he replied, "I suppose it could have been but if it was he was also carrying a suitcase and a load of perfume from downstairs."

So, having asked the divisional officers to stay by the entrance – both to prevent any escape but also to ensure Ronnie was not confused – we started our search in the basement and worked our way upwards from there. The first floor was rather spooky as this was both menswear and lady's fashions; as a result in the darkness all the mannequins looked particularly realistic and as we reached the top of the switched-off elevator Ronnie was really very confused indeed.

Anyway we eventually cleared this floor and headed upwards to the bedding department on the second floor. This time we took the ordinary staircase, as we knew this was the route our intruder had taken. I stood at the top of the stairs working out how best to search this floor, which of course was still in total darkness.

Suddenly out of the darkness came a voice from beside us: "Alright Butt, need a hand?"

Fortunately I still had Ronnie on a short lead and very much under control as we both nearly jumped out of our skins. It was one of the divisional officers who had obviously not understood fully my instruction to stay by the entrance. Still, he was with us now so I told him to stay by the door while Ronnie did his search.

Within seconds Ronnie started to bark, indicating he had found someone and my torch beam showed him barking at a large double bed, under which our fugitive was hiding. So the two of us joined Ronnie and together we hoicked out our intruder who made no effort to resist with Ronnie's breath just inches from his face.

So despite the ghosts, the mannequins and the errant copper we had made our collar but it had been quite a scary experience for us both.

PC Alan Hubbard

A car had been abandoned at the Maenllwyd Inn in the village of Rudry, a few miles east of Caerphilly. I and my dog Major had the job of finding the driver of this vehicle that had led some of my colleagues in Traffic a merry dance over many miles.

It was the middle of the night when Major and I took off

from the pub and it was clear to me that Major had a very definite scent on which to track. Now anyone who knows that area will know that it is a very beautiful part of South Wales with lots of rugged scenery – mountains, forests, streams and marshland. Our fugitive driver, who had been pursued for so many miles in the car, now decided to ensure that Major and I were also going to have to work hard if we were going to catch him.

He led us for quite a while along the Rhymney Valley Ridgeway Path, which was relatively easy, but once we were well south of Caerphilly he veered off across the fields heading towards Pontypridd. We crossed the A 468, the main road into Caerphilly and then we were tracking along with the busy A470 off to our left. We later worked out we must have tracked for over five miles and by the time we reached Griffin Mill, right beside the main road, both Major and I were absolutely exhausted and on our last legs. So I had called up reinforcements in advance and it was here that I met up with a colleague who was going to carry on the search.

I very quickly briefed him and Major and I were both delighted to go and rest in his vehicle as we watched him and his dog set off on the same track. They were still only a few yards from the van when his dog shot off to the left and started to bark at a hedge.

They had found our man only 50 metres away from us and after all that work they got to make the arrest. You win some, you lose some!

Until very recently most police dogs came from members of the public who donated them to us, usually because they found they were too much of a handful for them. On one occasion, a lad on my shift had collected such a dog and, to save taking him all the way to the Bridgend Centre, he called and asked if I could kennel him for the night. The dog started howling as soon as we put him in the kennels, I went to the pub for a bite to eat, came back and he was still howling. At about 2 a.m. it went quiet at last and I managed to get some sleep. In the morning, I came out to find he had completely destroyed the kennel and was no longer there. He hadn't gone quiet because he had settled down as I had thought; it was because he had escaped. I spent all day driving around the area searching for him, but this proved a little tricky, as I hadn't actually seen him clearly the night before so had no idea what he looked like!

At about 6 p.m., I was driving past a local pub and could see a man shooing away a German Shepherd from the front door with a broom handle. I stopped and said, "Excuse me but is that your dog?"

"No it bloody well isn't", came the quick reply.

"Well it must be mine then", I said as I caught him and put him quickly into the back of the van.

PC Iestyn McNeil

It was 2 a.m. when I was tasked to support some local officers in the St Fagans area of Cardiff. They wanted me and my dog Riley to help them find the driver of a stolen car that had crashed and overturned. The helicopter was already there and had found our driver down by the Ely River so, being guided by them, Riley and I set off in pursuit.

We soon had him in sight and when he saw us he decided to escape by swimming across the river. I shouted at him to stop before releasing Riley to bring him back to this bank. When he realised what was about to happen our fugitive stopped swimming and headed back our way. I recalled Riley and put him back on his lead. The man dragged himself out of the river and dripping with water he squelched his way along the bank towards us.

As he came alongside us Riley started to bark at him and at that moment he made a lunge at the dog and Riley responded by jumping up and pushing him back into the river. As he fell he grabbed me and took me with him so now both of us were up to our necks in the river.

Once again he pulled himself out on to the bank and tried to get away but from my very wet position I ordered Riley to detain him, which he did by grabbing him by the buttocks, at which stage our fugitive decided to give in. I now pulled myself out and with the help of my dry colleagues, who were finding it very hard not to laugh uproariously, he was arrested and charged with the theft of the vehicle, amongst other things.

Riley had a good towelling down when we got back to the van but I had to find a 24 hour store so that I could purchase a towel and some dry underwear. I spent the rest of my shift in my overalls.

Embarrassing Moments

There is an old adage in the world of theatre: "Never work with children or animals". This of course refers principally to their innate ability to steal the limelight but actors also have in mind their general unpredictability and inability to follow the script, no matter how well trained they might be. Police dogs are no different.

Everyone knows that the most anti-social aspect of dog ownership is the irresponsible owner who does not clean up after their dog has done its business in a public place. Police dog handlers also have to deal with this problem in many different environments.

PC Gareth Roberts

I, together with my drugs search dog Noddy, had been tasked to search incoming baggage for drugs at Cardiff International Airport. Realising that this would be a long job confined inside a building I had ensured that we had had a good walk on the beach at nearby Porthkerry. On arriving at the airport we went through all the various security checks to get to the 'airside' area and into the arrival hall where the suitcases were circulating on carousels waiting to be reunited with their owners.

A flight had just arrived from Bridgetown, Barbados, and there were some very smart designer label suitcases coming through the hatchway on the carousel. Noddy had done this before and was soon jumping between the Louis Vuitton, Samsonite and Mulberry suitcases without caring whether

they were genuine designer labels or counterfeits, picked up for quarter the price in some overseas bazaar. Suddenly I noticed that he had stopped working and had started the unmistakable circling action that preceded the inevitable act of defecation. In front of a large crowd of suntanned arrivals and while still circulating on the carousel, as if on a stage, Noddy let it all out. There was nothing I could do to stop it.

Being a very well trained and eager-to-please dog the moment it was over Noddy was back at work sniffing at the suitcases. I had to halt the carousel and much to the amusement of the passengers rather sheepishly had to clear up the mess. It did result in an ironic round of applause from all the passengers.

PC Mark Frowen

Late into a night shift I was tasked, together with my first and favourite dog Ben, to a bakery in Pontypridd where the alarm system had been set off. We arrived at the premises in total darkness and immediately found a window that had been smashed. Without the key holder being there this window was the only means of access into the bakery. Having cleared away the remains of the glass, I lifted Ben up and helped him through the window so that he could search the building and see if there was anyone inside. The window however was too small and too high up for me to get through so I could not follow him inside. Ben did his search in the dark and, when I called him back, he jumped up at the window and I caught him and pulled him back through. We returned to the van, reported that there was no-one there and resumed our patrol.

However very early in the morning the bakery staff turned up for work. They opened up the doors to find the unmistakable signs of dog mess all over the place. Ben had obviously been caught very short and I had had no idea. The staff had no option but to set to with their mops and disinfectant as they had left the premises immaculately clean and ready for their regular inspection by the Food Standards Agency. Unfortunately for them there were very few windows so, long after all visible signs had been removed, the unmistakable aroma of 'poo de chien' lingered on through the day. The manager of the bakery, although very grateful for the quick response to the alarm call, did find it quite difficult to explain to the food inspectors why there was this rather unusual non-bread-like smell.

Cardiff International Arena was hosting a gala night at which Pavarotti was performing and Princess Diana was attending. A large search team of four dogs was sent to check the building for explosives during the preceding afternoon. For this task I was using my search dog Skye, a large liver and white Springer Spaniel. Pavarotti was warming up in the auditorium during his final rehearsal as we arrived to start our search amongst the seats. We had only just started amongst the front rows when the great tenor's voice rose to some of the higher notes in his register. At this point Skye stopped searching, jumped into the air and started to howl.

Fortunately the big man found this very funny even though Skye's singing was hardly in harmony. Pavarotti's support team were not so amused so I decided to take Skye to another part of the building so as not to spoil the rehearsal.

So it was that we found ourselves in the call centre where 20 ladies were busy working the telephones as people rang in to buy tickets. Skye was much admired by them all but he, being very focussed on his work, kept his nose down and chased around the large room not letting them interfere with the task in hand. Suddenly Skye went into the only open patch of space in the centre of the room and started to circle round demonstrating quite clearly what was about to happen. Before I could do anything, Skye's rear end exploded with the foulest smelling diarrhoea. He managed to empty that room faster than any bomb threat. He was an explosive search dog in more ways than one.

PC Gareth Roberts

Some homes that the police have to enter leave a lot to be desired in the cleanliness stakes. One such house in Tylorstown was detailed off for me and Noddy to search for drugs.

In the kitchen there was a mountain of dirty dishes, old takeaway containers, and the occasional cooking implement piled up and filling the sink. The bathroom had not been cleaned for months. In all three bedrooms we found soiled mattresses and bedding, as the adults moved round the house rather than use the washing machine. The state of the house was not helped by the fact that there was a large Bull Terrier living here and it was obvious that he was not getting the necessary outside exercise in order to carry out his usual bodily functions. Consequently, scattered around the house were little piles of doggy-do, some of which had been there for ages and the smell of urine pervaded every room, where the poor dog had lifted his leg on the furniture because he could not get outside.

Nevertheless, while I tried hard not to wretch, Noddy carried out his task without being deflected by all these other very pungent aromas. It did not take long before he came across various drugs ranging from amphetamines through to a substantial amount of heroin. Most interestingly we came across the house vacuum cleaner, which had obviously not been used for years for its proper purpose. Inside the 'bag' was a sizeable stash of cannabis.

By now the two occupants had been arrested and were being held in a police van by other officers, all of whom were only too pleased not to spend another minute in this revolting atmosphere. We were left to complete the search on our own.

It was while we were in the last bedroom before completing our search that Noddy found the smells were all too much. I had somehow managed not to throw up despite it all but suddenly Noddy decided to demonstrate exactly what he thought of this utterly revolting place by adding to the piles of excrement with his own contribution.

I tried to clear it up but, after removing the worst of it, I decided that by the time the owners were allowed back into the house they would not be able to tell it apart from their own dog's mess. We both needed to get out of that hell-hole quickly before I made my own contribution.

PC Dai Conway

During the summer there are various shows around the South Wales area where the Dog Section is invited to lay on a full demonstration of its skills. One such display was at St Athan. Each handler was to take part in a different event ranging from simple obedience skills through to more demanding search and detain tasks.

The first team into the arena was myself and my dog Sam and together we marched in smartly with Sam demonstrating brilliantly his devotion to his Dad by walking, then running, at my heel.

Having made our way right into the centre of the field so that we had everyone's undivided attention it was the routine of 'down', 'stand' and then 'sit'. The first two parts of this well practised routine went immaculately then, prior to walking away, I gave the command 'sit'. On this command Sam, without any prior warning signs, promptly squatted and made a terrible mess in front of many hundreds of the good people of St Athan. It was at this point that the commentator, who had been explaining in great detail what the crowd had been witnessing, announced over the tannoy: "I thought I heard Dai tell the dog to 'sit'". By now the crowd was hysterical with laughter and I knew, even if Sam was oblivious to it all, that this would take a lot of living down amongst my colleagues.

PC Derek Francis

Another day, another demonstration. It was a very wet day when I was invited with my German Shepherd Bruno to a local infant school in Cardiff to show the children the various skills of a police dog. The school had planned for the demonstration to take place on the playing field but because of the weather the head teacher decided to move the event inside and had all the children sitting on the floor around the edge of the small assembly hall.

I came in with Bruno and introduced him to the children before explaining some of the many skills that were required of a fully trained police dog. Given the small size of the hall this was not going to be an opportunity to demonstrate the more aggressive skills but there was still a good routine to show off Bruno's amazing loyalty to me and his high standard of training.

After 10 minutes of explanation I decided to demonstrate some obedience skills. So I marched up the centre of the hall with Bruno at my heel, turned right, turned left and then did a complete about turn back to the centre of the hall. Three steps into that final manoeuvre I realised I no longer had Bruno at my heel. On turning to look I was horrified to see Bruno squatting and producing really disgusting diarrhoea all over the expensive parquet flooring.

The children looked on aghast and some began crying and saying they felt sick to their teachers. There was a real commotion in the hall. Needless to say South Wales Police Dog Section has not been invited back to that particular school. Those theatrical types were quite right: "Never work with children or animals" Certainly never with both at the same time!

The Amazing Powers of a Dog's Nose

Did you know that a human's nose has six million sensory receptor sites whereas a dog's has, depending on its breed, between 200 and 300 million? In addition that the part of a dog's brain dedicated to analysing those smells is 40 times larger than that of a human's? That is why humans around the world use dogs for their powers of smell. Emergency services use them for finding drugs, explosives, firearms, money and humans, both dead and alive. In addition dogs can be trained: to detect cancerous tumours, diabetes and epilepsy; to find truffles buried deep under the roots of trees; to find game birds while ignoring other animals and even to find vermin or mould.

Meanwhile humans have developed amazing technology to help them and a police search team has a whole array of equipment, all highly expensive and prone to technical problems (including flat batteries!), to assist them in their work as dogs may not always be available when they need them. But no matter how sophisticated the equipment no-one has yet developed anything with the power and sensitivity of a well-trained dog's nose.

PC Richard Heath

It was just after midnight when I was asked to help in the search for three high value shotguns and some ammunition stolen from a house during the previous day. Shotguns can range in value from about £100 to many tens of thousands of pounds; to a copper the value is insignificant, they are all equally lethal when used by a criminal. So finding stolen firearms is always a high priority and the Force Technical Search Team had been deployed, as a result of some intelligence, to a large area of waste ground behind a vast block of flats. The area was very overgrown and included four derelict, burnt out outbuildings in various advanced stages of decay and knee deep in debris. The entire surroundings were heavily covered in brambles with only a single muddy track though them.

The search team had covered the area as well as possible over a long period using metal detectors and other equipment but in the dark they had found absolutely no sign of anything untoward.

I went to see the senior detective who told me how much work they had put in to searching the area and all to no avail and so, having had a quick walk round the area to check for any hazards which might endanger my search dog Cracker, I returned to the van and harnessed him up. I worked out a methodical search pattern and we started right alongside the block of flats, which seemed as good a start point as any.

I was however rather worried about the huge amount of broken glass that littered the ground as dogs' paws and glass do not really mix well. So I tried to keep Cracker very much under control and used my powerful torch beam to direct him. For ten minutes we worked our way across the open ground and into the first outbuilding. Cracker very quickly told me that there was nothing here and we moved on to the next. He was way ahead of me into this building and by the time I caught up with him he had completely frozen and was indicating at a burnt out wooden cupboard. I struggled to make my way through all the debris and rubbish that covered the floor to a considerable depth and joined him. I only had to lift a couple of pieces of burnt plywood from the base of the cupboard unit to see three gun cases hidden beneath them.

I dug into my pocket for a treat for Cracker and shouted out to the search team leader for them to join me. They made

PS George Fortey and Police Dog Bess, 1962.

An early operational Police Dog and crime fighting duo.

Farro and Murphy.

PC Paul Krauze and Cody overcome the simulated wall jump.

Cody.

Fleeing 'criminal' PC Gareth Jones gets stopped in his tracks by Finn at Firearms Training Exercise.

PC Steve Atkinson apprehended by the flying dog Zeus.

PS Andy Patterson's screams or gun don't deter Police Dog Axis.

PC Ian Hemburrow and Charlie.

The chase.

The reward after the chase.

PC Bob Woolford and Finn.

PS Justin Watts and some young new recruits.

PC Bob Woolford and Tye.

PC Sally Richards and Nikita on the scent.

PC Dave Smith and Farro.

PC John Hughes and Max.

PC Leighton Andrews with Police Horse Danby and pups Woody and Norman (now both drugs dogs).

PC Dave Smith and Murphy find a real stash of drugs in a dry stone wall.

PC Dickie Wiseman and Joey working at Cardiff Central train station.

PC Gareth Jones and Victim Recovery Dog Badge (working in water).

PC Ian Hemburrow and Roxy and PC Kevin Hughes and Zeena with their combined haul of silverware from Trials of 2012 (Zeena 1st Welsh National Champion after 53 years).

Our finest three new recruits: PC Chris Francis and Viper, PC Steve Bowen and Van, PC Russ Jones and Archie, PC Rob Jones Instructor and CI Belcher.

Competing in National Trials.

Animal Welfare Officer Paul Watkins shares a tender moment with Dutch.

Inspector Hobrough and a switched off Lady.

PC Ieuan Evans and Ben.

Dutch.

PC Emma Viant and Deana.

Top Team at Wood Green's Open Day 2013. Back row left to right – Nerys Baker and Dennis Baker of Wood Green, PC Andy Goodall, Author John Gaye, PC Leighton Andrews, South Wales Police Volunteer Matthew Rees, PS Andy Patterson. Front Row – PC Bethan Jones, PC Mike Newman and Badge and PC Steph Llewellyn.

their way over and having taken the necessary photographs for evidence we eventually opened the cases to find three very beautiful, very valuable and immaculate shotguns inside. Sadly there was no sign of the ammunition so Cracker and I carried on searching but eventually I decided to call it a day as there was so much glass about and I did not want to push our luck too much and risk cutting Cracker's paws.

It had taken less than 15 minutes for Cracker to find these guns; the search team, with all their kit, had been looking for hours.

PC Mel Pascoe

At some stage in our lives we have all read about, or seen on the television, the sniffer dog being given an article of clothing before heading off to track down the owner successfully. In reality it is not quite like that. Frequently search dogs have only an abandoned car or a doorway from which to identify a specific human scent and then to follow it, ignoring all the other human (and animal!) smells that pervade and corrupt the start point and the ground over which the target has gone. It never ceases to amaze me how they do it but they do, so just as with my computer, I only work on knowing how to use their powers rather than worry how these powers work.

We often get sent to abandoned cars, frequently after they have crashed, to pursue the driver and any passengers. It was one such incident to which I was sent in the village of Ynysybwl, which is at the head of a small valley just to the north of Pontypridd.

When I eventually got to the scene of the accident I found a Ford Focus which was completely wrecked as it had hit a wall at speed and the nearside of the car was an awful mess. But I quickly found the lovely lady who had reported the accident and she told me that she had seen the driver and his woman passenger head off towards the centre of the village.

Having put my dog Cassie into a harness we set off in the direction the lady had pointed out and immediately Cassie had a scent on which to track up the street.

As it was late on a Saturday night, just after the pub had closed, there must have been many other people along this street quite recently. There was plenty of evidence of the revellers going home in the form of chips dropped along the pavement and Cassie, while not losing focus on the pursuit, enjoyed the odd snack as we proceeded.

Eventually we arrived at the front door of a terraced house and Cassie indicated quite clearly this was where our fugitives had gone. Just at that moment the local divisional police told me on my radio that they had received a call in the last five minutes from the owner of the car, reporting it stolen. It seemed that the owner of the trashed car just happened to live at the address outside of which Cassie and I were standing.

So it must have been quite a shock to the owner when I knocked on his door just minutes after his phone call to tell him we had found his car and that we knew that he had been driving it, and could prove it, when it crashed. I breathalysed him in his hallway and he was way over the top so I arrested him and he was successfully charged with drink driving.

But I was really pleased with Cassie's track as there must have been so many distractions on that pavement, not least all those delicious chips that she had enjoyed. She still got her treat but rather less in her bowl at her next feed.

PC Derek Francis
We have to search for drugs in many different types of house. Sometimes the house may be immaculately furnished and spotlessly clean, at other times it may be astonishing that anyone can live there. The house we were sent to in Porthcawl,

with a search warrant for drugs, was definitely in the latter category. The smell hit you the moment you went through the door; the smell of stale fried food, unwashed kitchen utensils and rotting takeaways permeated the whole house and I knew our clothes would reek of it for the rest of the day.

The warrant had been served earlier that morning by the leader of the search team and although they were convinced that their intelligence was sound they had found no drugs. After two hours futile searching with all their equipment they had called for me and my dog Kobi to help them.

It was only a small terraced house so it did not take long for Kobi to search the ground floor, without any result. Together we climbed the stairs and went into the first of two bedrooms. Within a minute Kobi started to bark at the frame of the double bed indicating strongly that he had found something significant. The focus of his attention was the brass knob on the frame. So very carefully I turned the knob only to discover it was easily removable and inside the brass bed frame we found what we were searching for – lots of cannabis.

For the rest of the day I could detect the smell of that revolting house on my clothes; how on earth do dogs cut through all those diverting smells to pinpoint so accurately the smell of drugs?

PC Ian Hemburrow

It was in the summer of 2008 when I was called to the village of Nantyffyllon, deep in the valley to the north of Maesteg, to support local police officers who had discovered cannabis being grown in industrial quantities in a disused public house. They had been there since early morning having served a search warrant and having found row upon row of cannabis being farmed in the building. But although there were signs of occupation and they had spotted, very briefly, someone round the back of the building when they arrived, they could not find any occupants anywhere inside.

So I put my dog Charlie into his harness and we started our search, working our way up from the ground floor. It was only when we got to the top floor that he started to indicate the presence of people. However it was one of the last rooms in the house to be searched and, on the face of it, it was completely empty. Indeed it was empty of everything including furniture. I was about to tell my colleagues that there was no one here. I tried to get Charlie back to the doorway where I was standing but he kept on showing an interest in the far corner.

Having faith in my dog, an important factor in our working relationship, I decided to investigate further. The walls were just made of plasterboard, which were easy enough for me to smash open with a good kick. Having pulled away the boarding I discovered one rather frightened man hiding in an alcove behind what had been the wall. But there was absolutely no access from this room.

Our fugitive had accessed his hiding place through a tunnel that led up from the second floor. This tunnel also led to another alcove behind the wall in the other corner of the room and in here we found another very frightened young man.

Both men were arrested on the spot. It is all very well finding and destroying the cannabis factory but without capturing the people responsible not a great deal is achieved apart from a minor delay in the production line.

Charlie was the hero of the day and I basked in his glory. What an amazing nose he has!

As well as Charlie, who is a general purpose dog, I also work with Max, who is my drugs search dog. It was Max whom I used to assist in the search of a house belonging to a well-known drug dealer in the small town of Rhoose, near Cardiff International Airport.

The divisional search team had already been through the house but without any success. However they were convinced that there were drugs in the house but just too well concealed to be found without a dog. Max quickly got to work and very soon he had searched the ground floor and we were upstairs in the master bedroom.

It was very obvious to me that the owner seemed to use a lot of cosmetics and deodorants, judging both by what we had seen in the bathroom and the vast amount of talcum powder that was evident in his bedroom. The smell was also quite overpowering. But Max had interests other than the suspect's toiletry habits; he was much more interested in a computer tower that was on the floor under a desk.

So having pulled out all of the connecting wires I pulled out my trusty Swiss Army knife and carefully unscrewed the front of the cabinet. Hidden inside, and there is often a lot of empty space inside a computer cabinet, were four golf ball size lumps of base amphetamine, all wrapped up inside a smelly old sock.

All these perfumed distractions had not fooled Max.

Neither did they fool him a few days later when we were tasked to search a Ford Mondeo, which had been stopped by traffic police in suspicious circumstances in the small town of Pyle, near Bridgend. The officers on the spot were convinced there were drugs in the car but had not been able to find anything in the usual hiding places.

Max jumped on to the driver's seat and instantly started indicating at the steering wheel. So we pulled out the dashboard, which gave us access to the steering column, and it was in here we found 4 bags of amphetamine and 20 tablets of ecstasy. Job done.

Another 'result' by Max was in the Cardiff suburb of Llanrumney. This was an immaculate house, more like a show home rather than the usual dives we more often have to search, and Max had almost immediately sat down in a corner of the kitchen and was staring up at the very expensive corner cupboard units. So I opened up the cupboard and brought out numerous plastic containers with all sorts of different foodstuffs inside: breakfast cereals, rice, pasta and such like. I only had to open up four boxes before I found one that contained 40 individual packets of cocaine, 40 'deals' ready for going on the street. No wonder this was such a smart house.

PC Mike Newman

There had been an armed robbery in a betting shop in Aberdare. No-one had been hurt but there had been many rather frightened and very angry punters who, although they had probably saved a lot of money in the process, had not been able to place their bets and had to go home frustrated. The robber, obviously trying his best to blend in with what he considered was the 'local look', had worn a wig, dark glasses, a leather jacket, a cricket cap and gloves. Having taken some few hundred pounds in notes from the terrified bookie's assistant behind the counter he had headed off into a nearby park and this area had been sealed off overnight waiting for specialist search officers, which included myself and my dog Sprout, to attend the next morning.

Sprout set off across the park and very quickly found a leather jacket, matching the description, in the long grass.

From there he headed straight to a dustbin and tried to get into it. My initial thought, somewhat unfairly in retrospect, was that Sprout was scrounging for food but, overcoming my doubts, I decided to have a look. Inside the bin was a large plastic bag that contained all the suspect's clothing – glasses, hat, gloves, wig and his trousers – together with a plastic handgun and some 'bullets'.

We left them where we found them, wondering what he was wearing to go home in, and carried on searching for anything else that he might have jettisoned in his semi-naked flight. Sprout finally located a yellow rubber band from the roll of bank notes and shortly after I decided the whole area had been comprehensively covered.

The Scene of Crime Officer could now retrieve all this evidence, which we had left in situ and take it off for detailed forensic science examination. As a result the culprit was identified from the DNA left in the clothing, he was arrested, went on to admit to the crime and was sent down. The good punters of Aberdare were once again able to lose their money to the bookies and the bookies were able to keep it safe for themselves.

PC Richard Heath

Some of my police colleagues in the Cardiff Drugs Team, while patrolling in the City Centre, had stopped and searched a man whom they suspected strongly of being a dealer in some of the nastiest of drugs. As a result of the body search they found some cannabis on him, which allowed them to mount a search of his home. Thus it was I was asked to support them with my drugs dog Cracker. When I got to the address in the Ely district of Cardiff I found that the drugs team was way ahead of me and had already searched the house unsuccessfully. This house was newly built, very well kept and had a patio and lawn with gravel borders.

I decided to quickly search the garden before heading inside. But we had hardly got going when I realised that Cracker's behaviour was such that he was on to something. He continued to quarter the small garden and then froze with his nose directly on a section of stone chippings between the garden shed and the boundary wall. He would not budge; he was staring at the ground so intently.

This told me all I needed to know and I was immediately alongside him on my hands and knees digging furiously into the gravel and mud with my bare hands. Having cleared the gravel I had gone down over six inches into the soil before I came to two large clear plastic bags containing over 100 'deals' of crack cocaine and heroin.

For the public of South Wales this was a really significant find and as a result Cardiff was now short of another loathsome drug dealer. For Max it was also hugely significant because this was definitely his best ever find. A really brilliant example of what a dog's nose can achieve.

The Chase

Being a dog handler requires the police officer to be agile, fleet of foot and physically fit. Although there will be a few occasions when it is physically impossible to take the same route as the dog, the handler will normally keep the dog on the harness so wherever they may be tracking he must be able to keep up with his fast four-legged friend. This may take them over ploughed fields of heavy clay, up or down steep embankments, over walls, barbed wire fences and electric fencing and sometimes up, or down, the mountains that dominate the northern part of the South Wales Police Region.

Fortunately criminals are rarely very athletic and are often burdened with their loot but when there is 35 kg of ferocious dog following you at speed it is amazing what can be achieved physically while attempting to flee.

PC Sam Dunstan

It was very late into a night shift when the call came through and I was actually in the centre of Cardiff. Apparently there had been a burglary in the Merthyr Tydfil area and, surprisingly, I was the nearest dog handler to the incident. Even though it was 5.30 in the morning, and I had my blue lights flashing, it still took me and my black sable German Shepherd, Yatz, 40 minutes to get to the scene, where a local officer was waiting to brief me.

This was a new estate and it was one of the most recently completed houses which had been broken into whilst the elderly occupants were asleep. However they had been woken by the sounds of the break-in and the husband had gone down to confront the intruders. Fortunately the two men decided to make a run for it rather than assault the elderly man. As I spoke to the officer the owners came out of the house in their dressing gowns and slippers, visibly upset, still shaking and clinging to each other for support. My heart went out to them. Their beautiful new home had been broken into, their treasured possessions rifled through and some of the more valuable stolen. Their security and their privacy had been violated and they felt vulnerable and helpless.

The local officer explained that by now over an hour had elapsed since the two burglars had made off. The tone of his voice was apologetic, feeling sorry for having dragged me all the way up from Cardiff and feeling that he had wasted my time. I looked at the old couple on their doorstep and felt that I must try to do something. In my heart of hearts I honestly believed that I would just be taking the dog for a walk, but it was worth a try.

I opened the back of the van and let Yatz out of the cage. "Show me where you last saw them", I said to the couple. The gentleman took us to the end of the street and pointed towards the right. "Has anyone else been down this way?" I asked the Merthyr officer. "No, we waited for you" came the reply.

As I put the harness over Yatz's head and lifted his front paw through the leg piece, the dog was already searching for the start of the track, stretching out his neck and moving his head from left to right sniffing at the air. I buckled him in and picked up the line. Clicking the catch onto the harness, I whispered "Seek!". Yatz immediately jumped forward in the harness and moved through the darkness along a pathway towards an area of the estate that was still in the process of being developed. Just short of the security fencing that was surrounding this area Yatz turned right and went into a small courtyard with large wheelie bin storage areas; here he made a left turn, and another and then came back out onto the pathway we had first turned off. At this point I was starting to think that the Merthyr officer had told a little white lie and that he had walked round this courtyard, but with that unworthy thought, Yatz pushed round the edge of the fencing and really started to put all his weight into the harness. My colleague had decided that he was coming with us and was close behind. Yatz was nose down, straining into the harness like a sled dog, almost pulling me off my feet. The 30-foot line was tearing through my hands burning my skin. And Yatz had started to whine, a familiar sound when he was on to the quarry.

Yatz tracked across the building site, through mud and trenches, ready to be laid as footings for houses; then, on reaching a sheep netting fence at the boundary, jumped over without hesitation, still straining against the lead.

Handlers have to be able to keep up and at the same time be able to spot any subtle changes in the dog's body language so that they can read their intentions. Perhaps it's the adrenaline pumping, or the thrill of the chase, or just that the dogs pull the handlers faster than they can run of their own accord, but there is nothing like it, and tracking is definitely an art form.

The early hours of that February morning were pitch dark. As Yatz tracked I had to put my total trust in him. He pulled so hard into the harness that I had to brace against him, leaning back in order to stay on my feet. Each foot fell on to unseen, uneven ground. Yatz jumped forward into the harness time and time again, frustrated at being held back, whilst I struggled with the fences and obstacles that Yatz found so easy to negotiate. After jumping the fence Yatz moved through the trees and undergrowth. The hawthorn and blackberry barbs caught in his coat and pulled at my uniform and cut into my face.

The ground started to rise and got steeper and steeper

until the next thing I knew we were on a dual carriageway, the A470. Yatz then crossed the central reservation. He jumped both metal barriers. "Wait" I shouted. Yatz hesitated, clearly not happy at my lack of agility, but having to jump two metal barriers, three foot apart, at speed needs to be done a little bit carefully.

Yatz then tracked across the A470 and down the opposite embankment, again pulling through trees and undergrowth. On the far side of the embankment was a quiet lane with a footpath heading towards a gated field. Yatz crossed the lane, turned right and headed towards the gate. I could see in the surrounding area that we were heading towards another housing estate. Yatz popped through the gate, forcing me to use the 'wait' command again to give me a chance to climb over it.

By this time the Merthyr officer had caught up with us again. I explained to him that I believed that we were on to something and joked that if it was a fox we were following, I would have Yatz's guts for garters! We crossed the field and came out over the gate on the other side. Here Yatz slowed down to a steady trot, concentrating on the hard surface and concrete under his nose. By this time Yatz and I were both exhausted. We had travelled for well over a mile, over rough terrain in the dark and cold and now we were struggling. "Come on son", I thought "Don't fail me now."

Yatz then dropped down into a culvert filled with water and took a drink. That's it, we are finished – I thought. Embarrassed, I turned to the poor officer who had followed us and told him I thought we had lost the track. Thankfully the Merthyr officer had been updating the other officers in the area with our whereabouts and the area was crawling with police vehicles. With that Yatz finished his drink and came out of the culvert, put his nose to the ground once more and continued to track.

This time he was different. He was methodical and moved slowly. I failed to read this having not seen him like this before. I went with him initially, but when he started to head back the way we had come, down over the fence from the A470, I started to doubt him. During the many years I had been a dog handler, I had learnt not to try and think for the dog. Even an experienced handler cannot know, or even hope to know, how a dog thinks when he is tracking. He is an instinctive hunter.

He does not rationalise. He deals in fact. Is there scent or not? He never wonders 'maybe they jumped into a passing car' or 'maybe they have found a bike and have ridden off' or 'maybe a passing alien has abducted them'. The dog is either on the track or not. The scent is either there or not.

Yatz, tired and frustrated from dragging me for over a mile or so then jumped over the fence and started to climb back up the embankment of the A470. At this point I made the fatal error of not trusting my dog 100%. I convinced myself that Yatz had somehow picked up our inward track and was now back-tracking. How could the track go back the way it had come? Who, in their right mind, runs from the police and then goes back towards them? I put the brakes on. I stopped Yatz and recalled him. He jumped back over the fence and, all too weary from the track, willingly obeyed.

We then slowly walked back the way we had come along the path towards the culvert. Not knowing the area at all, we made our way back in the direction where I believed the burgled house was located. We crossed under the A470 at an underpass. Here Yatz started to change. His whole demeanour and body language changed. His head came up and his tail arched over his back as he started to pull me towards the embankment.

Then I heard the sound of someone crashing through the undergrowth, up on the embankment. I shouted towards the noise in the undergrowth, "Police dog. Stay where you are!" and unclipped Yatz from his harness and the dog, at last released from having to pull his Mum along, jumped over the fence into the undergrowth. The poor dog was totally engulfed in the blackberry and hawthorn bushes, the thorns bit into his coat and held him fast. I climbed over the fence and tried to free him but I too became caught up in the thick undergrowth. I took out my baton and hacked at the bushes. They seemed to come alive and to grab at us both, hindering our every move. Eventually we both managed to get through the thick bushes and found ourselves back on the A470. Yatz piled straight into a large patch of bracken and started to bark. He had found one of the burglars lying face down. The other one had run off back across the dual carriageway and been lost.

The man in the bushes was arrested and taken back to Merthyr Police Station.

All the property from the burglary was recovered, a TV, a laptop and a purse. But also items from another burglary on the same estate were found in a wheelie bin in the courtyard from where we had first started tracking.

If I had gone with Yatz, and trusted him when he jumped the fence back onto the embankment, we would have had both fugitives. But hindsight is a wonderful thing. If only I hadn't thought that I knew best. On returning to Merthyr Police Station, the adrenaline subsided and every muscle ached in my body. I went into the Ladies to tidy myself up and looked in the mirror. My face was bloody, my uniform was torn in many places and my cheeks were bright red with the cold and effort. I looked at myself and smiled. What a buzz. What an absolute rush. I washed up and went out to the van, opened Yatz's cage and gave him a bowl of water. "Well done old friend", I told him. "Sorry I didn't trust you, it won't happen again".

The Stupidity of Some Criminals

There are, no doubt, many criminals who are extremely clever; however they tend to be the ones we never meet because they do not get caught. Indeed the really clever criminals will only commit crimes that are never detected in the first place. Fortunately for the police there are many criminals who are definitely not from the brightest element of society and whose simple errors ensure that they do not soak up too many police resources in their detection and prosecution.

PC Dai Brake

I was tasked, together with my dog Tye, to a burglary in the small Valleys town of Mountain Ash; it was 3 a.m. in early February and there was a good covering of snow on the ground. On our arrival I was briefed by the local divisional officer before getting Tye out of the van. Very quickly he picked up a track, which led down the main road for about 70 metres before going up an embankment and on to a disused tram track. We followed along this track before climbing another embankment and on to another road where Tye lost the scent. However we had discovered a very distinct and fresh footprint in the snow on the tramway – first error.

I then heard on my radio that the owner of the premises had a CCTV covering the property and our intruder was very clearly visible on the recording, carrying a rather distinctive bag – second error.

So, with Tye, I went back to the old tram track and re-started our search, this time looking for the bag, just in case in his haste he had jettisoned it. He had – third error.

As we walked along Tye indicated something half way down the embankment and on closer inspection it was a small black and grey backpack, similar to the one on the CCTV. Strewn around beside the bag were various personal items, one of which was a wallet enclosing various papers identifying the owner as a well-known local burglar – fourth (and mega) error.

So at 5.50 a.m. I found myself standing at the back door of a house in Matthewstown while the local divisional officers knocked on the front door. True to form the back door opens and our suspect tries to make off through the garden. I immediately issue a challenge and let Tye off his lead as our fugitive takes off at great speed – fifth error.

However at the same moment one of my fellow police officers comes out through the kitchen door, casting a great deal of light into the darkness of a cold winter's morning, which totally disorientates Tye whom I have to call back to my side to prevent him attacking my colleagues.

But once order is restored I release Tye once more and he jumps into the adjacent garden and immediately starts to bark indicating he has his quarry. I join him and find our suspect lying face down in some household waste like the proverbial ostrich – sixth error.

He is still wearing the same distinctive clothes he was seen wearing in the CCTV footage. So we now go back into the house, find another man together with some Class A drugs. We arrest both of them and eventually charge them for 3 burglaries as well as with possession of the drugs.

A very successful night's work although not too demanding on the 'little grey cells' thanks to the ineptitude of our rather stupid young man.

PC Ian Hemburrow

It was in the middle of a thoroughly cold and wet night in January when a householder in Penarth reported a burglary in his garage and I, together with my dog Roxy, went to investigate. We were there about 40 minutes after the owner had heard the break-in so I thought there was a good chance that Roxy would be able to track successfully, at least as far as the location of the get-away car.

It took seconds for Roxy to pick up the scent from the garage and she headed off into the adjacent lane before turning right, going up a flight of steps and out onto a terrace. She then tracked only for about 50 yards before turning into a yard and up to the front door of a house.

I could not believe that someone would commit a burglary so close to their home and not consider the possibility of a police dog being used to track them down. But the track had been very definite and just to compound the stupidity of the crime I could see a couple in the front room of the house, with the lights on and the curtains drawn back, surrounded by electrical equipment.

I called for some back-up and when my colleagues arrived we banged on the door, which resulted in the man attempting to escape through the window. He however, spotted Roxy, who was now ready to complete her evening's work with an arrest, and decided instead to run upstairs and hide. It was not a difficult task for Roxy to find him hiding in a cupboard.

We also found six lawn mowers, a strimmer, a gas heater and five gas barbecues. Our not very bright suspects also admitted other burglaries in the area.

PC Ieuan Evans

The small rural village of Pyle lies between Bridgend and Porthcawl, not far east of Port Talbot, and is not the sort of area where you would expect an armed robbery to take place. But I was sent, together with my dog Dylan, to the local garage to investigate just such an event. Apparently a man had threatened the duty attendant with a shotgun and had then made off with all the cash in the till. When we arrived it was only about five minutes since this had happened so I got Dylan out of the van and he immediately followed a track up the road and then into a housing estate.

But it was just as we came to a halt that I heard on my radio that a taxi driver had called the station to report having picked up two men from this area and he was very concerned about their conversation. It seemed that our culprits were escaping the crime scene by taxi – a rather unusual method of get-away car – and the driver had sent us their destination address.

We ran back to the van as fast as we could and set off to the address the taxi driver had provided while he took the slow route there. Meanwhile the Armed Response Unit was able to get in position before the taxi arrived.

A short while later the two men were seen on foot approaching the address and, when challenged by the armed officers, one of them stood still while the other attempted to run off before Dylan caught him and he sensibly decided to stand still until arrested. It was their first sensible decision of the night.

PC Terresa Sullivan

A burglary had taken place in a house right out in the countryside to the east of Caerphilly and an Audi A4, together with its keys, had been stolen. The following night the car was spotted moving in the Llanrumney area of Cardiff. As a result an extensive search was mounted to look for the car, which was spotted once again, this time heading towards the Trowbridge area where eventually a local unit found it parked up in a small cul-de-sac.

I arrived there with my dog Luca and together we started tracking from the car. Luca led us along a path between two houses and we ended up outside the door of No 4. This was all we needed to be able to make a forced entry to the house. Inside we found four men, who all had stacks of form for burglary and theft. We arrested them on the spot but to strengthen the evidence we needed to find the keys to the Audi as an additional link to the crime.

We searched high and low throughout the house; we searched thoroughly each of the four men but after an hour we were about to give up when one of the divisional officers, who had been outside to his car for a moment, came back in to tell us that the Audi's lights kept flashing as it was being locked and unlocked by someone.

So we went back to our four suspects, all of whom were being held in the kitchen while we searched, and searched them again. One of them had been clever enough to conceal the Audi electronic fob in his hip pocket which had been missed on the initial body search. But he was stupid enough to lean up against the kitchen units and thus had been locking and unlocking the stolen car. We had our evidence.

One Man and his Dog

Before any officer can join the Dog Section they must have proved themselves on the beat as competent in the many skills that are required of any police officer. Although in the Dog Section they will be trained to utilise the many inherent attributes of their dogs, they are still very much required to exercise their extensive experience and knowledge to ensure that they get the very best out of their canine partners.

Teamwork, between Man and his Dog, is vital in all operations in which they are deployed. So often local knowledge, common sense or some forethought and planning can ensure that the dog's chances of success are multiplied many times over.

PC Bob Woolford

It is all very well identifying from intelligence the principal drug dealer in an area; it is often a very different matter trying to catch him. The higher up in the drug dealing food chain they are, the more difficult they are to implicate and charge.

We all knew the identity of the main dealer in North East Swansea and the Regional Task Force had carried out many searches of his property over the months, all to no avail other than to inconvenience him. No drugs or excessive amounts of cash were ever found either in his house or on his person. He was very careful in everything he did.

However whenever he was spotted by a police officer, a report of the sighting would be made and sooner or later something significant would be forthcoming. And one day someone saw his vehicle parked up away from his home and next to some woods. It was only there for a short time before he emerged from the woods and drove away. There was absolutely no evidence of anything untoward, he may have just stopped for a pee, but I was tasked to investigate with my dogs Tye and Toby. So this unusually is a tale of one man and his two dogs.

I arrived where his van had been parked within a short time of his departure and Tye, my general purpose search dog, quickly picked up the track into the woods from that spot. I followed him, together with Toby, my drugs dog, until we arrived at a copse of trees, which seemed to mark the furthest point of his track into the wood.

Now I deployed Toby to search the area for drugs and within a couple of minutes he started to indicate the presence of narcotics buried in the ground. This turned out to be a large plastic bag containing many smaller bags of amphetamines. But not content with this, we carried on casting around the area and soon Toby was indicating again; this time he had found 15,000 ecstasy tablets, which we also retrieved.

But it is all very well finding the 'stash', what we really wanted was the dealer so that we could remove this dangerous offender from the community for a good long time. Having safely removed the drugs, we returned the scene to normal, ensuring that all traces of our presence were carefully eradicated. This then allowed some of my colleagues to mount a discreet watch on the area for when he returned.

It was only 24 hours later before he came back into the woods and he got the surprise of his life – actually, two surprises. Firstly he discovered his precious commodity was no longer there and secondly he felt the long arm of the law reach out and grab him.

As a result of this relatively simple operation, many more dealers were identified and arrested and considerably more drugs were found and seized, thus reducing a significant proportion of Swansea's supply and suppliers of illegal drugs.

PC Steve Atkinson

This is a story of two men and two dogs, but all working as a team and using local knowledge to ensure no one escaped.

I was tasked to what was reported as a burglary in process at a large garden centre in Cardiff. But I reckoned that by the time I got there the burglars would be long gone and finding a track in an area so well trodden by hundreds of people would be nigh on impossible. But I had a hunch that I knew to which local estate they would be heading, so quietly and discreetly I made my way there where I met up with my fellow dog handler PC Geraint Bruford and his dog Ronnie.

I had parked near a subway and path that led from the garden centre and very shortly I spotted in the distance a man coming down the path carrying some boxes of garden equipment. Geraint and I agreed that he would make his way with Ronnie to the other side of the subway so that he would be on the same level as our suspect and would be able to cut off his retreat.

They were only about 10 yards apart when Geraint shouted his challenge: "Police with a dog: stand still or I'll send the dog". At which stage our suspect dropped all his boxes and sprinted off down an adjacent lane. Ronnie gave chase and very quickly leapt up and took our fugitive down on to the ground.

The man continued to fight off Ronnie but when Geraint told him to stop struggling and he would call off the dog, he did but only long enough to try to take off once more. Having felt Ronnie's ministrations a second time he gave in completely and Geraint could now handcuff him and take him away.

I, meanwhile, from my well hidden observation point, had spotted two more men, clutching garden equipment, coming our way and it was clear to me that they were totally unaware that their mate had just been arrested. I waited until they were right beside me before stepping out of the shadows with my dog Dave tethered close by my side. I too challenged them and they were so surprised, indeed totally shocked, that they immediately lay down on the ground as I requested.

Together, using some local knowledge, the four of us (two men and two dogs) had caught all the burglars red-handed and the garden centre soon had all its stolen goods returned to them.

It was way back in 1993 when I was sent with my dog Rocky to University Hospital in Cardiff where the security guard had reported two men breaking into cars in the car park. When we arrived I met up with the guard and, as he took me and Rocky round to the area where he had seen them, I let Rocky off his lead to see what he could find in the dark.

Rocky had disappeared round the back of the building when two youths broke cover about 150 metres from where I was standing and headed off towards an adjacent lane. I called out a challenge for them to stop, which they ignored, so I called Rocky back to go chasing after them.

The youths disappeared out of sight with Rocky in very close pursuit so it was not long before I heard that familiar and very welcome sound of Rocky barking and a man letting out a frightened scream. I quickly caught up with them and told the youth to stop struggling. But as I approached him to detain him he pulled a large screwdriver from his jeans and threatened to plunge it into either me or my dog if we came any closer.

This screwdriver was of sufficient size that it could do either me or Rocky a great deal of damage but neither of us were prepared to let this young man escape, so I stepped forward with Rocky beside me to disarm him. With no warning, and before Rocky could do anything about it, he brought the screwdriver down, aiming at my chest, but I managed to deflect the blow with my arm. Even so, it managed to penetrate quite deeply into my left arm near my elbow. But he had made his move and with the help of Rocky and the security guard, who had come to help, we got the handcuffs on him before he could do any more damage to any of us.

Despite being cuffed this angry young man continued to be extremely aggressive to all of us and his violence carried on even once he was in custody.

Once local officers had arrived and taken him away I could step inside the hospital and have my arm looked at by a doctor. If you are going to get stabbed by a criminal where better than in a hospital car park?

It was about 4 o'clock in the morning when officers spotted a stolen vehicle in the St Mellons area of Cardiff and started to pursue it. The stolen car was being driven pretty recklessly so the officers held back and just monitored where it went. It was heading eastwards out of the city.

Eventually, monitoring the chase on the radio, I heard the pursuing officers cackling with glee as the stolen car had turned down a long road called Hendre Road and, providing they did not turn off it, they were going nowhere as the road ended at a lake. The driver of the stolen car obviously had no idea where he was going so when he rather abruptly reached the end of the lane he managed to crash the car. Three men got out and the passengers, who were rather shaken up by the crash were immediately arrested by the pursuing officers who had closed in on them when it was clear they were beyond the built up area and were no longer a danger to the public.

But the driver high-tailed it and the torches of the divisional officers picked him out wading the lake and heading to the island in the middle. At this stage I arrived with my dog Rocky and together we set off in pursuit. I wondered why our fugitive decided to head into the lake; did he think that no sensible police officer would want to follow him into the water at 4 a.m. in early April? How wrong can you be?

The lake was not particularly deep so I could wade out but Rocky had to swim, which didn't worry him. As we waded and swam across my torch beam played on the island where I could see our man watching our progress and, as we approached him, he made off to the other end of the island which was all of about 200 metres long. I shouted out a challenge to him to give himself up but he obviously decided to ignore this so I sent Rocky on ahead to detain him. That was all that Rocky needed to take off after him. Immediately I released him from his leash he powered ahead and very quickly he was on the island running at speed across it.

As I pulled myself out of the lake I could hear Rocky barking and the man screaming in fright. He was obviously not going anywhere and very soon I was alongside them and found the man with his hands round Rocky's throat trying to ensure he was not bitten again.

By now my dry colleagues back on the south side of the lake had called for reinforcements, who arrived on the northern side so we only had to wade about 50 metres from the island to the north bank where they could arrest the driver.

It turned out that these three men had been involved with various burglaries around the city as well as the theft of one written-off expensive car.

PC Steve Atkinson received a Superintendant's Commendation for this particular arrest.

PC John Johnson

I happened to be patrolling in my van in Cardiff, quite close to the City Centre, when the call came through on the radio telling us all that there was a man right in the heart of the shopping area threatening people with a handgun. So it was that I was first on the scene and as I drove up, aiming to meet with the Firearms' Officer so that we could concoct a plan, I spotted the man walking into the middle of the street and pointing his pistol directly at the driver of a Ford Mondeo, who had to swerve to avoid knocking him down.

The gunman then walked back on to the pavement and approached a Ford Ka in which a rather pretty woman was sitting in the driver's seat having pulled over to chat on her mobile phone. She was so intent on her call that she failed at first to notice the man pointing a gun at her; when she did she had the presence of mind to immediately put the car in gear and she drove off at high speed.

While I was watching all this go on I was parking my van and extracting my dog Millie from the back. So far our man had yet to spot me. By now I realised that there was no time to find others, this man was posing an immediate danger to the public and we had to intervene immediately.

So with Millie on her leash close by my side I approached the man, shouting at him to drop the weapon. You often hear soldiers say, when interviewed after being involved in a battle: "Oh, the adrenaline and the training just kick in." That was how it was with me. I suppose, in retrospect, I could say that my heart was in my mouth as we walked down that pavement but all I could see was a man threatening members of the public for whose safety we were responsible. No-one, I felt, had the right to be threatening so many people in the very heart of our city.

After I had shouted at him the man looked at me and, now ignoring everybody else, started to walk towards me with the gun still in his hand. I was just about to release Millie when a couple with three children in tow walked round the corner and directly into the line of fire. I screamed at them to move away and the husband grabbed all three kids and they disappeared back round the corner.

But now the man had raised his gun and was pointing it directly at me from about 30 metres distance; he could hardly miss so I put my hand on the release of Millie's lead. But just at that moment the man dropped his weapon on to the pavement. That had been quite some scary moment and I let out a huge breath of relief. Millie and I continued to advance towards him and the man now reached inside his jacket; with that I decided once again to release Millie to grab him.

She tore forward, faster than I had ever seen her in training so she knew this was for real, and he now produced another handgun from his jacket pocket. But instead of pointing it at anyone he carefully placed it on the floor beside the other weapon and put his hands in the air.

With that I decided that he had given up and recalled Millie. By now she was travelling at speed and as I called she was just about to launch herself at him. 40 kg of Alsatian at 30 mph would certainly have knocked him over on to the floor and taken the wind out of him. But she was such a well trained and brilliant dog, on the point of launch she spun round and returned to my side; her bum just made contact with the man as she turned.

With that I shouted to the man to lie down which he did and I quickly handcuffed and arrested him.

The guns actually turned out to be very realistic replicas

but to me, and to the others whom he threatened, they looked very real indeed at the time. We had often trained for this situation but those soldiers are right – the adrenaline and the training do kick in and take over. But what they do not tell you is what happens once the excitement is over. The knees knock, the hands shake and you need to sit down fast as the adrenaline levels fall, and the reality and the dangers of the situation you have just faced hit you.

For this incident PC John Johnson received the Operational Police Dog Incident of the Year award for South Wales

PC Richard Heath

It was 2 o'clock in the afternoon in January when I heard that police officers in the Llanrumney area of Cardiff had spotted a man whom they knew was wanted on an outstanding warrant and, when he had seen them, he had run off.

I was monitoring all this on my radio as I headed towards the area to help them catch him. I could hear that the helicopter had been alerted and now had spotted our fugitive heading towards the river and the dual carriageway that leads out of Cardiff, the A48.

I thought there was little point in trying to catch our man by following him from where he had started; not least I felt certain he was about to swim across the river and I could see no reason why I and my dog Ozzy should get wet unnecessarily.

The helicopter now reported that our man was swimming the river and was heading in the general direction of the Pentwyn area. So, using my local knowledge, we headed across the bridge over the A48 and turned down the lane called Church Road and parked up discreetly at the Unicorn Inn. From here, and guided by the reports coming from the helicopter, Ozzy and I walked down the footpath, along which I was told our man was coming towards us.

Suddenly there he was, only 20 metres away. I told Ozzy to sit and shouted my usual challenge to this man who was by now sopping wet and very cold from his river crossing in mid winter. All the fight went out of him and he surrendered immediately. It was our arrest but Ozzy and I were just part of a team all working together. Thank goodness I knew of the Unicorn Inn from the occasional visit, off-duty of course!

It was just after we had handed over our very wet and cold prisoner to local officers that we heard on the radio about another incident, very close by in the St Mellons area. The report came from a man who claimed that he had been seriously threatened by a group of men in a white transit van. They had threatened to stab him and had then thrown knives at him before heading off. He knew the names of some of them and I recognised the names when they were repeated; I knew them too and they were not a particularly nice bunch of guys. So I decided to patrol the area on the look out for their van.

It was not long before I spotted their vehicle coming towards me and pulling an old caravan. As I rapidly did a U-turn I got permission from the incident commander to approach them if possible. So I followed them discreetly until I saw them pull over in the street. Two blokes got out and started to fiddle with the tow-bar. Four other men, who were standing around on the pavement, struck up a conversation with them. This was not a nice area and, as I needed reinforcements if I was to make any arrests, I played it very cool indeed. I pulled up behind them and, having opened up the rear door of the van so that everyone knew I had dogs with me, I approached the two passengers asking them about a tail-light on the caravan which was not working.

This seemed to allay any suspicions that my interest in them was anything other than for a minor traffic infringement. Meanwhile in my radio ear-piece I could hear that the armed response unit was approaching the area fast. I continued to walk round the vehicle and the caravan and by now the driver had stepped out to join us on the pavement.

Then suddenly they were there; the cavalry had arrived in an unmarked police van. The firearms unit jumped out and arrested the two passengers while I slipped the handcuffs on to the driver.

But by now the street was beginning to fill up with people who had been alerted that we were making arrests and the atmosphere was turning very nasty indeed. Fortunately at this moment reinforcements in the shape of some local officers appeared on the scene and we could withdraw safely from the area with our prisoners.

We had got the right men and they were subsequently done for violent disorder.

PC Sam Dunstan

It was Valentine's Day just before midday when two men were seen breaking into a house in the St Mellons area of Cardiff. They had made off on foot and local officers had quickly arrested one of them but the second one had managed to get away.

Dante and I were only a few minutes away so we were quickly at the spot where the man was last seen. After a brief search a second call came into the control room from a member of the public reporting that a man was hiding in her garden.

Dante and I made our way to the address and I told Dante to search. I watched him as he picked up a track, scaled the fence into the next garden and jumped up onto his back legs bracing his front legs against a 6 foot high garden wall. Being an old dog, he tried his hardest to get over without any likelihood of success. I went up to the wall and using a nearby garden chair, climbed up on top of the wall and sat astride it. I called Dante up to me and, as he jumped, I grabbed his collar and helped him up. I pulled him across my knees and settled him down as we had done many times before, letting him relax and take a breather. I looked down and checked the landing side of the wall was clear of any danger and then, when he was ready, I let Dante jump down. Dante had jumped down into an alleyway between two gardens. I followed and put him onto his lead.

Dante then tracked along the alley, nose down on the hard surface pathway. He tracked out of the alley and across a main road and on to another path that headed up to a small housing estate. As we tracked along together, another call came in from a member of the public reporting that a suspicious man had been seen running into the area of Courtney Close. I looked up at the sign on the wall and realized that we were entering Courtney Close.

Dante tracked into a garden of the Close and pulled me into the flower beds and jumped up on the back fence. I climbed up on to the fence and saw that there was at least a 20 foot drop into bushes in the garden backing on to it. There was no way I was going to ask Dante to jump down into that. I looked long and hard into the garden below for the man we were following but he was nowhere to be seen.

I counted the roof tops of the adjacent street and counted four houses from the left. I pulled Dante reluctantly away from the fence and we ran as fast as we could back to the dog van. Dante jumped in and looked at me as if to say, "What the hell are you doing?"

I drove around from Courtney Close, and into the street

that backed onto it. As I drove into this street, I counted the roof tops of the houses and pulled up outside the fourth house in. I quickly ran to the back of the van and Dante jumped out, eager to continue his search.

We ran up the driveway and up to the side gate. It was locked. What should I do now? I knocked at the front door praying there was someone in, as there was no car on the driveway. My luck was in!

The house owner answered the door with his two-year-old daughter in his arms. I apologized profusely and asked if I could possibly get into his garden. I explained why and he allowed us through the house, which was a large detached house with the most fantastic open plan kitchen I had ever seen. It was immaculate, with oak panel units, granite worktops and a really fancy tiled floor.

By now Dante and I were both really muddy and I apologised for both of us as we left our own tracks across their kitchen and out into the garden!

We went through the kitchen and out through the patio door and into the garden. Here I slipped Dante from his lead and instructed him to search. I could see the bushes and the 20 foot high fence at the back of the garden and knew we were in the right place.

Dante spun around the garden and went towards a shed. He went up to the shed and started to whine and scratch at the door. He looked at me with a "Come on, open the door" look on his face. I walked up to the door of the shed and saw that there was a small hook and eye catch on the top that was engaged and in place.

My human, logical thinking brain, told me that there was no way anyone could be inside the shed as how could they lock themselves in? Every bone in my body, every logical thought in my brain, told me there was no way there was anyone hiding in that shed. I looked at Dante, my wonderful, faithful, trustworthy friend and said "Ok, we'll check this, just for you"

I flipped the catch and looked inside. The shed was filled with various items of garden furniture, old cushions, deck chairs and cardboard boxes. I put Dante on to the lead and started to move items around. I moved a large cardboard box from the back of the shed and saw a rather ashen-faced burglar, hiding under the boxes.

He looked up at me and I think our surprise was mutual. He was just as shocked to see us as we were to see him. Dante started to bark, as if he was saying "I told you so Mum!"

I arrested the man and as I pulled him to his feet he let out a scream. He had broken his ankle jumping down the 20 foot drop into the bushes. So together we had got our man. Dante needed me, both to work out which garden we had to go to and to open the door of the shed; I needed Dante to show me where the man had gone and where he was hiding. We made a good team together.

The Softer Side of Police Dogs

Occasionally the South Wales Police Dog Section are invited to various events as part of a public relations exercise in order for the public, the vast majority of whom would never get to see police dogs in action, to learn more about what they do. For some of these events it is sensible just to take the more docile specialist search dogs so that the public can meet them close up without any concerns for their safety.

PC Alan Russ

Because I was one of the more experienced dog handlers I often found myself, during the latter years of my service, being sent to these events with my two dogs – Pippa and Wilkin. Pippa was an extremely bouncy Springer Spaniel and Wilkin was an equally energetic and restless Border Collie. As both dogs were normally hyperactive, sitting or standing still for any length of time was not really in their nature, particularly when they were 'on duty'. But they did enjoy the attention of people and had spent some very happy hours being petted by hundreds of children and adults although neither really settled down to make it easy for me or for their adoring public.

One lovely summer's day I was tasked to attend the Open Day of Tŷ Hafan, a local children's hospice. As usual we had been approached by nearly everyone who was attending the event; neither dog had given any trouble but both had been as hyperactive as always, bouncing around, jumping up and generally not settling down.

Then a lady approached holding the hands of two rather fragile looking small children, a boy aged about 4 and a girl aged

about 6, both in-patients of the hospice. As they approached, both dogs changed entirely from their usual frenetic state and sat down quietly so that these two small, very delicate people could hug them and pat them without being knocked over. To make life easier for them Pippa rolled over on her back to have her tummy rubbed and Wilkin swiftly followed her example. They stayed like this for over 5 minutes until the children decided that enough was enough and moved on. A few seconds later both dogs resumed their usual frantic bouncy state. What was it that the dogs had sensed in these two very ill and delicate young children? Whatever it was, it had helped to make those kids' afternoon really special.

Each police dog has its own individual character. Some are naturally excitable to a level where the handler has to remain extremely cool, often in testing circumstances, in order to maintain essential discipline. Some are particularly highly prey-driven and enjoy the chase and the reward at the end of it, so require a very strong handler. But because they all have to undergo a rigorous training schedule and are assessed at every level before they are

allowed out on operations South Wales Police ensure that dogs and handlers are well suited to each other.

However 'General Purpose' police dogs are not generally known for their cuddly nature and the breeds chosen for this particular discipline have to be strong, brave and intelligent. Mostly they are selected from the various types of European Shepherd dog or Alsatian. There are also some Rottweilers and Dobermans that have served SWP well over the years and should not be forgotten for their valuable contribution. In a similar way, specialist search dogs need different attributes. They need a good nose, masses of enthusiasm, boundless energy and, of course, like their larger more robust colleagues, a great deal of intelligence and a willingness to be trained. Hence these dogs are chosen from the breeds that are genetically programmed for these skills: Spaniels, Labradors, Collies and Pointers predominate in these roles.

PC Mark Frowen

Ben was my first dog. He was a Belgian Shepherd, all 35 kg of him, bursting with energy and always ready and willing to do whatever his Dad demanded of him. But he had no great love of those he met while in the line of duty. Indeed he gave the impression to everyone who met him when he was working that he was not to be petted or even approached by strangers. However every day, after work was over, I would take him home with me and he had the run of the house until bedtime when he was placed in his kennel.

It was early days in our partnership when I learnt how I could trust Ben totally with my family. It had been a long and very busy Saturday night shift with a great number of incidents at which we had been deployed to deter drunks from violence and to encourage them to go home peacefully. Twice Ben had been ordered to detain over-aggressive young men who had threatened me or my colleagues with violence.

As a result two men had been arrested before being taken to hospital with bites on their arms or legs. We returned home exhausted and I put Ben to bed in his kennel before retiring to bed myself.

I awoke at lunchtime, had a shower and came downstairs to find my two daughters had let Ben out of his kennel and he was having a great game with them in the garden doing various obedience tests and retrieving old tennis balls that they had found amongst my training kit. Ben was enjoying himself enormously, not least because he was getting considerably more fuss made over him than he was accustomed to.

Both children had been brought up with dogs and had no fear of them. In turn Ben recognised familiar smells and two young people who posed no threat to him. He seemed to recognise that he was not on duty and he could relax and enjoy himself. Although I had not planned this particular unsupervised encounter it gave me great confidence in my dog's ability to understand, rather like a well-trained guide dog, when he was on duty and when he could relax and enjoy the company of humans without any aggression.

Over the years Ben would join the family in various activities. In the winter we would all go sledging on the nearby hills and he even learnt to pull the toboggan up the hill before chasing the kids down to the bottom.

In the summer we took him with us on our camping holiday. All the kids on the camp site loved Ben and enjoyed telling him what to do. As he was trained using hand signals, not just voice commands, I could stand behind the child and, as they told him to 'sit', I would point to the floor so that he sat immediately. The kids thought it was really special that this huge burly police dog would actually listen to them and obey their commands so well.

One year, while travelling in South Devon, we even entered

him, probably rather wrongly, into a dog show's obedience classes where he swept the board. It would have been rather embarrassing if he had failed to win.

Sadly Ben died when he was 13 and for the whole family it was as if some close relative had passed away. He had been a great companion to me when we shared many hours together on duty, he had been loyal and brave in protecting me and my colleagues in various violent situations but above all he had been part of the family to us all at home.

PC Gareth Jones

In the spring of 2004 I was working with a German Shepherd dog called Sumo. I had had him for about a year and a half. One day I was in the police station in Treforest, enjoying a cup of coffee at 3 a.m., when a call came out for a burglary in Porth, just up the road. I dropped everything and dashed up there. When I arrived, local officers told me that they could hear people moving about down in the bushes by the river, so I went there first with Sumo. There were police everywhere and we thought we had the area pretty much contained. A few minutes later, another officer said they could now hear noises in some bushes that ran alongside the road. I worked my way up the river bank, towards the road and Sumo was about two metres in front of me. Out of nowhere a van came round the bend and hit Sumo. The van came to a stop about 30 yards further up the road; the driver got out and said, "What have I hit?" Apparently he had seen all the police but not Sumo, a dark dog on a dark night.

Sumo was underneath the van and I crawled underneath and pulled him out. He was dead. Sumo was a big dog but I managed to pick him up and I carried him back to the dog van and put him in the cage. I drove to a nearby car park, stopped the van and went round the back and opened up the boot. I was talking to him, "Come on Sumo, good boy, up you get then." I knew he was dead but I was in shock and I just wouldn't accept it. He was just lying there and had blood coming out of his mouth.

I drove to a vet in Cardiff and started banging on the door. Of course no one answered, as it was four in the morning. So I got back in my van and drove to another vet in Merthyr Tydfil, banging on the door. Again there was no reply. So I went home. I was so shocked and distraught I didn't know what I was doing. I waited up until 7 am when I contacted my Sergeant and told him what had happened.

Sumo had made the ultimate sacrifice in the line of duty and I had lost my friend and partner.

PC Cliff Piper

Ben had served me well as my General Purpose police dog and together we had had some fantastic results; finding prisoners, controlling football crowds and protecting me in some fairly hair-raising incidents. He was always raring to go and showed no signs of slowing down. But then there were two separate incidents that caused me to start questioning him.

The first was a burglary at a rugby club. The alarm had gone off and when I got there, I got Ben out the van and walked around the building checking all the doors. As we came to the front, the door burst open and a male ran out. I sent Ben to detain him. The male turned left out of the gate and I lost sight of both him and Ben. We had recently been issued with new body armour and I was struggling to run in it and catch them up. As I got to the top of the hill, I came across Ben, just sat there, panting. The male was nowhere to be seen. I couldn't understand what had happened, as Ben had never, in all our years together, failed to catch someone before, let alone just sat down.

The following week there was a car chase in Llandough and I managed to tag onto it. A short while later the car crashed and there were two occupants out and running. A divisional officer managed to grab the driver and I sent Ben to bite and detain the passenger who had pretty much run straight past my van. He was only 10 yards away but Ben just ran alongside him and didn't bite him. I could hear all the officers at the scene saying what a rubbish dog I had, but I knew it wasn't true. I knew Ben was a brilliant dog.

So a few days later I took him to the vets to get him checked out. The vet diagnosed a crumbling spine and that the bones were pinching on the nerves. I had had no idea. He hadn't let me down at all; he'd been in too much pain to do what I'd asked of him. But he had always tried, always wanted to please me. The vet said he had a week left. I thought he meant by that comment a week left in 'work' before I'd have to retire him, but no, he meant a week left to live. I was devastated. I decided to take him home to spend some time with him but he rapidly went downhill. I made the heartbreaking decision to have him put down only days later.

The Force Multiplier

There are many technical devices to make the work of a single police officer more effective and thus give a law enforcer the essential advantage over the individual determined to break the law. These devices obviously include the various weapons ranging from the basic baton, through the Taser to eventually the whole range of firearms, which are only deployed against specific threats. Other devices include simple pieces of equipment such as handcuffs, radios and protective gear and, more technically sophisticated, computers with their massive databases and a whole range of clever things like heat-seeking cameras on helicopters.

But perhaps one of the most effective, simple and obvious 'Force Multipliers' to enhance the capabilities of a single police officer is the dog. The police dog can not only search out a whole range of items, often faster and more efficiently than a complete search team equipped with the very latest technology, it can also multiply the physical threat of a single officer to those intent on breaking the law. Few violent criminals are likely to be so stupid as to take on one or more highly trained General Purpose police dogs.

PC Emma Viant

It was just after chucking out time in the pubs and I was patrolling Cardiff in my vehicle accompanied by my dog, Deana, when the call came through. There had been a racially motivated attack by three men on a vehicle and its driver in the area of Pentwyn in North East Cardiff. As I was on Eastern Avenue at the time it was a matter of minutes to get there and, as it is an area I know well, I could anticipate just where these three very drunk and unpleasant young men might go. I parked up, extracted Deana from her cage, and together we hid at the end of an alleyway which I was convinced would be their route home. I struck lucky. Within a couple of minutes I heard voices approaching but we continued to hide in the bushes until I could positively identify that they matched the descriptions I had been given.

There were only two of them but I was convinced these were the same two violent youths who had beaten up the poor driver for no other reason than his ethnicity. Deana and I stood up and confronted the two men with Deana making it quite clear that she was really keen for them to try something. They sobered up rather quickly and very shortly I had handcuffed them both before calling for back up from the local officers. But then my luck held because, despite all the noise from Deana a third man turned into the alleyway. In the darkness, and no doubt hindered somewhat by alcohol, he failed to appreciate what was happening and it was only when I challenged him that he turned to run away. Despite his drunken state he was sensible enough to realise that he could not out-run an angry German Shepherd so he quickly joined his two mates and five minutes later the local officers arrived and all three were carted off to the local nick.

Could I have stopped them on my own? Without Deana I would probably have ended up in the same hospital as the unfortunate victim of this unprovoked violence. As with so many other similar incidents one well trained dog can provide sufficient potential threat to the violent criminal that even when drunk they come quietly, even for a 5' 7" police woman.

It was just before Christmas and round about 3.30 p.m.; it was both cold and getting dark when I was sent to the Splott area of Cardiff with my dog Comanche. I was part of a larger team, including a helicopter, in pursuit of two men, both wanted for various crimes and both listed as being potentially very violent, who had been spotted making off through various back gardens in the area.

So as a team we started methodically to work our way through the gardens in the dark. Overhead the helicopter was hovering, all the time watching for movement and also using its thermal imagery equipment which highlights very clearly on a cold December evening any signs of humans concealing themselves where they might not be otherwise seen.

My radio crackled into life and, listening closely to the report from the officer monitoring the thermal imagery in the helicopter, I realised he was reporting a significant heat source in the large shed in the adjacent garden to where I was standing.

Comanche and I quickly jumped over the fence and broke into the outbuilding, which was chock full of various discarded pieces of household furniture with a double mattress piled on top. By now Comanche was really excited and I felt certain that inside this pile of jumble at least one of our fugitives would be hiding. I stood by the door and called out my challenge before releasing Comanche from his harness.

He immediately started to climb up the mattress and, just as he reached the top, two men stood up and immediately surrendered. I called on Comanche to return to me and ordered the two men to come out. They both complied with amazing speed, no doubt encouraged by the dog's aggressive barking by my side, and within seconds they were handcuffed and waiting for local officers to arrest them.

It was only after they had been arrested and taken away that I was told that these two local villains were well known for their violence and they were wanted on suspicion of various serious offences including assault, burglary, possession of drugs and not least breaking the terms of their parole from prison. I also discovered much later from another dog handler that one of these men had been bitten twice before by Comanche on previous arrests and he was now terrified of him. No wonder he gave himself up with such alacrity.

PC Dave Smith

It was 4.15 in the morning of an August Bank Holiday Monday and the clubs of St Mary's Street in Cardiff had done a very good night's business. But they were now closing and encouraging their customers to go home. Fuelled with alcohol many had decided to extend their night out by continuing to party or fight in the street. There was broken glass everywhere and a great deal of noise from some very inebriated people.

Although the local officers had deployed just about everyone available to enforce some order they were in danger of being overwhelmed. A number of officers had been assaulted and already there had been 10 arrests. This was the rather chaotic and extremely noisy scene that greeted me and my dog Farro as dawn was breaking on our arrival. The first thing we encountered was a very drunk woman acting very aggressively as she abused the three officers trying to restrain her. So with Farro closely under control on his harness, I went forward to try to act as some form of deterrent in order to encourage her to calm down. However on seeing us she kicked out with her bare foot and hit Farro in the jaw. Now this is not the way to make friends with a German Shepherd, least of all a police trained one. As she kicked again Farro only just missed grabbing her foot in his mouth, which was extremely fortunate for her. However her pre-occupation with Farro, whom she perceived as the main threat to her well-being, allowed the other officers to restrain her properly and she was bundled off, no doubt to repent of her night out later in the morning.

This allowed me to accompany three other officers to assist them in the arrest of a man suspected of dealing drugs in one of the clubs. I stayed just outside of the main exit from the building, ready in case the suspect tried to make a run for it, which he did.

The suspect had broken free from the three arresting officers and as he exited at speed, Farro, who was still on his lead, lunged forward and managed a good bite on his upper thigh. However the suspect decided that he would retaliate by punching Farro as hard as he could on the jaw. This did not improve Farro's opinion of the man; being punched there twice in one night was really beginning to upset his otherwise placid nature quite seriously.

While I released Farro from his harness the man dived into the crowd that were still milling around the street, swiftly pursued by Farro who now had but one thought on his mind. Ignoring all the drunks in his way he weaved round them and quickly caught up with our fugitive, who now decided to stop and face up to us. By now Farro was really fired up and he launched himself into the air and 35 kilos of furious German Shepherd knocked the suspect to the ground in a tackle worthy of the finest ever seen in the Millennium Stadium or even the Arms Park. The stupid man was still not prepared to give in and continued to kick out at Farro, who responded robustly by biting him on the chest and stomach.

My three colleagues by now had caught up with us and once I had called a very reluctant Farro back to my side they could continue with their arrest, no doubt calling into the hospital on the way to the nick.

But we were still surrounded by our Bank Holiday revellers, who seemed to see this as an additional entertainment for their night out. Indeed a number of them attempted to 'help' until discouraged by Farro's far from friendly demeanour. Unbelievably, with Farro back in his harness and under control on the leash, two very drunk girls, tottering on extremely high heels and in the sort of skirts that could also double up as pelmets and who had watched all the very violent action, decided that they would like to stroke Farro. Conversely and equally bizarrely there were a few drunken men who wanted to try their luck with Farro; they were discouraged by other officers who sent them on their way.

It had been a busy night but with Farro's support the local officers had managed to contain the trouble while managing to make an important arrest and without calling for reinforcements from elsewhere. Farro had a split lip, which quickly healed, and I gave him some very special extra treats at the end of our shift. I was very proud of him.

PC Mark Randall

The supporters of Millwall FC have a certain reputation, which tends to attract trouble wherever their team happens to be playing. Therefore when they were playing Cardiff City there was a definite plan to ensure the supporters were escorted safely from the railway station to the football ground and back again at the end of the day.

Escorting and controlling football fans is an expensive business in terms of manpower as the potential for trouble is considerable. To ensure order with the minimum deployment of officers, dogs are used to provide that force multiplier effect. Thus I found myself with my German Shepherd, Ally, being part of the 'bubble' which surrounded about 200 Millwall fans to escort them in safety to their penned off area in the ground. But along the route an ambush was launched by certain Cardiff City fans. Both sides were taunting each other to get stuck in and all were intent on proving just how 'hard' they were. The Cardiff boys however had to get past the police bubble in order to launch their attack.

They kept running up towards Ally, hissing at him, trying to wind him up even further even though he was straining at his leash, barking, growling and trying to bite any person who came within his range. But then one fan, perhaps with more Dutch courage inside him than his colleagues, got very close and slipped over. This was too much for Ally who proceeded to grab him by the seat of his pants.

Reluctantly I commanded him to leave the boy and pulled him back. As I did so Ally brought with him most of the fellow's trousers.

The last I saw of this fan was a very bright white bum with four very prominent and obvious bite marks as he limped back into the safety of the crowd. This had been witnessed by many, a lesson had been learnt and funnily enough no-one else from either side tried to taunt Ally again. The rest of the day passed off peacefully and I cannot remember who won on the pitch. Outside the ground the definite winner was South Wales Police Dog Section.

PC Chris Edwards

It was New Year's Eve and four of us dog handlers had been exercising our dogs and having a cup of tea in some fields at Gwaelod y Garth, just to the south west of Caerphilly, prior to what we thought would almost certainly be a busy night for us, when the call came through. There was a break-in in progress at Treforest Industrial Estate, just five minutes up the main road from where we were. We all piled into our vehicles and headed north.

We were the first police to arrive and we found the gates to the compound to the old factory were locked and bolted.

With the aid of some bolt croppers we gained entry and round the back of the building we found a small crowd of about 250 young people, unloading equipment and generators from about a dozen vans. They did not give us a very warm welcome, indeed they were positively hostile to the idea that they should pack up and go home. There was little New Year goodwill in evidence.

It was not long before other party-goers started to arrive in large numbers and fortunately the local Divisional Commander was very quickly on the scene so that he could read them all the necessary notice requiring them officially to leave the property. Once this notice had been delivered we could be rather more robust in our encouragement for them to disperse. But no doubt considerable effort and money had been invested in this planned 'rave' and there was now considerable hostility to us from what was an ever-increasing crowd of already inebriated and fired-up young people, who had made their way to this spot to celebrate the arrival of the New Year in style.

Because of its relatively remote location, away from large urban areas, there were still only very few police officers on the ground but we had four general purpose police dogs to support our six local divisional colleagues and us. That was all we needed.

We deployed the dogs and suddenly there was rather less hostility to us as the crowd recognised that you cannot rationally argue with or try to sweet-talk a 40 kg German Shepherd. They could begin to see the futility of trying to resist further. It took about two hours to clear the site completely but we managed it without having to call for extra help.

Afterwards we estimated that there had been over 2,000 people attending the party; they were dispersed by ten police officers plus four dogs. How's that for value?

The Thrill of the Chase

Police work, as with the work of all the emergency services, can be very tiring if there is apparently nothing much happening; patrolling in a vehicle in the middle of the night with very little traffic on the road and everyone else seemingly tucked up in their beds fast asleep.

Then suddenly everything can change and officers can find themselves in life threatening situations with more excitement and adrenaline running than is probably healthy for them. For officers in the Dog Section this frequently comes in the form of a chase with all the thrills that have excited Man since the time of the Flintstones. It is no coincidence that so many 'action' films feature at least one thrilling chase, by car, by boat, in a plane or on foot. Police officers in the South Wales Police Force Dog Section get the thrill of the chase for real on a regular basis.

PC Gareth Jones-Roberts

It was the start of a night shift in mid summer for me and my dog Ella. We were both not long out of police dog training school but we had trained together for some 3 months and had established a mutual trust and a wonderful working relationship. Just as we were starting out on a routine patrol the call came through – there was a burglary actually in progress at a house in Port Talbot.

That is one of the most exciting calls to receive because it means that potentially someone is still inside the property and if we as a team do our job well we can catch the burglar red-handed.

We headed to the address as fast as I could manage, remembering to shut off both the blue light and the siren well before we approached the property. As we arrived I discovered the local officers had positioned themselves both at the front and the back of the house so if somebody was inside they could not escape. I did a quick recce before getting Ella out of the van and discovered that both the garage door and the rear kitchen door were missing and that the neighbour could still hear noises coming from inside the house.

With Ella I approached the kitchen door and shouted out my challenges: "Police officer with a dog. Come out now or make yourself known to a police officer or I will send in my dog", which I repeated twice more to ensure that some poor innocent house owner was not going to be attacked by my dog inadvertently. However this house looked very much un-lived in and there was no response from inside. I set Ella off on her first operational search in a house. We were both very excited.

As we made our way inside I was reliant on Ella's skills as the whole property was dark, damp and lacked any form of electric light. It rather resembled an old haunted house with little nooks and crannies everywhere. This was for real and what a brilliant house to search.

Ella started her searching, going in and out of the various ground floor rooms, with an intensity as if she could tell that someone had been there very recently. This in itself heightened the tension within this dark and creepy building. However, within only a few minutes, Ella returned to my side to indicate that the ground floor was clear.

So I sent her up the stairs and I followed. The staircase creaked on every step and cobwebs caught in my hair and on my clothing. Just as I reached the top Ella came out of the first room and into the next. In the torch light I saw immediately her demeanour change, her chest puffed out and her ears pricked up even further. She knew, and was telling me quite clearly, there was someone in here with us.

In the middle of this otherwise empty room was a large water tank around which the floorboards had been lifted exposing the copper pipes underneath. Ella went up to the tank and immediately starting barking. That was all I needed to know and, having looked inside, I found a man lying flat on the floor of the tank. I invited him to stand up, which he did with alacrity and I handcuffed and arrested him before searching him. In his pocket I found a fairly substantial knife which could have caused a great deal of damage to anyone he chose to attack.

As we made our way out of the house with our prisoner I tried very hard to pretend to my divisional colleagues, waiting outside, that this had been just a simple routine operation, the sort of arrest Ella and I did every day. But inside I was bursting with pride. This had been our very first operational arrest and it had all gone so perfectly. I put Ella back in the van and drove away. We only got as far as the nearest open field, where I could park up and spend some time giving her all the praise and adulation possible. I wanted her to know just how chuffed I was with her. I think she got the message.

PC Dave Smith

In the middle of the day I was sent, with my dog Farro, to a house in Trealaw, near Tonypandy, where there was a report of a man strangling and beating up a woman. As I was in the middle of Cardiff and Trealaw is half way up the Rhondda Valley it took us nearly half an hour to get there; so it was not particularly surprising to learn that both people had long since left the house. But there were others living in the house, the same people who had called for police help, and they described the man, told me what he was wearing and that he had left through the rear garden. That was all I needed to set Farro off in the right direction.

He immediately picked up a track, heading through the garden and then down into an alleyway, which ran behind the property. I had little enthusiasm for this particular chase as, since it was just after noon, there was bound to be serious contamination from the general public who had walked along this route since our man ran down it. Also I was rather distracted by having stepped in some other dog's mess and was busy trying to remove it from the soles of my boots. But Farro was focussed on the track and was pulling me along the alley. We had hardly gone 100 metres when a man, exactly fitting the description we had been given, stepped out in front of us. I could not believe our luck. Suddenly we had a very real opportunity to make an arrest. The day had brightened up considerably.

I shouted to the man our usual challenge, encouraging him not to run away but rather to give himself up at once before I released the dog, but to no avail. He ran off at great speed and now my exhilaration was getting Farro even more worked up. In my excitement I gave him every known command that I had ever used and Farro lunged forward whipping the tracking line out of my hand. Fortunately I had worked with Farro for over 2 years and he really needed no detailed instruction from me. He knew what he was doing despite his 'Dad' losing all his self-control in the heat of the moment.

He followed the man who rather stupidly ran into a small cul-de-sac where he tripped up and fell over, smashing a glass that was in his pocket. Farro was right alongside him almost immediately and although completely tangled up with his long lead wrapped around his legs he contained our fugitive long enough for me to catch up and handcuff him.

It had hardly been a textbook pursuit but despite being the

middle of the day and despite all my over-excitement Farro had done all that was required of him and we had our 'collar'.

PC Sam Dunstan

We were two days short of Christmas and it was 4 a.m. when I heard on my radio details from the Traffic Inspector who was following a car, stolen earlier from Caerphilly, but was now in the Thornhill area of Cardiff. It was a fairly long chase which ended eventually back in Caerphilly where the car was abandoned on the top of the mountain. The passenger was arrested on the spot but the driver had made off into the nearby fields.

I had, needless to say, been following all this on my radio and had decided to head up that way in case I and my dog Dante could help out. So we arrived only about 10 minutes later and the Inspector could point us in the direction that the driver had taken, over a five bar gate and into a field. I smiled to myself and thought "Great – a lovely grass track".

It was freezing cold and pouring with rain but that never made a difference to Dante. Even in high winds it just meant that he was a few feet off the track with the wind. I put Dante over the gate and harnessed him up. Dante went left and right and then settled down into his usual tracking mode. Head down, nose to the ground, and loping along steadily.

As we started to track across the field I realised very quickly that it was a ploughed field. The mud was so deep it was almost half way up my shins and Dante had to lunge forward and back in order to keep moving forward. Despite this he kept going and we made our way across the field.

Half way across Dante hesitated; I looked down and saw a white training shoe sticking out of the mud. One of the traffic officers had followed me into the field and I shouted to him to pick up the trainer, as I believed it belonged to the car thief.

Sure enough a few metres further there was another trainer. The male was now running barefoot! How perfect is that for a dog to track. Not only is the track on earth but the person making off has no footwear. The scent must have been even stronger for Dante to follow.

We crossed the field and came to a barbed wire fence. This stuff is evil and can open a dog up easily if they don't jump it cleanly. Dante stopped at the fence and started to whine. I knew that he wanted to go over the fence but was unsure of the wire. I looked over the fence and saw that there was thick undergrowth with blackberry bushes the other side. So thinking I knew better than the dog I took him off his harness and line believing that our man must be hiding in the undergrowth.

I shouted a challenge, my usual challenge when sending the dog to search. I said "Police with a dog. Come out now or I will send in the dog" I placed my leg out horizontally on top of the barbed wire and commanded Dante to jump. He jumped over my leg and landed in the undergrowth. The poor dog immediately became tangled in the blackberries and had difficulty moving. I jumped over the fence and took out my baton and started to chop at the undergrowth trying to make it easier for the dog to work through. I still believed at this point that the man must be hiding as the undergrowth was so thick.

Dante pushed through and all went quiet. I waited in the bushes for him to bark after finding our fugitive but nothing came. After about five minutes I started to panic. It was a foul night, lashing with rain and wind and it was freezing cold. I started to think that perhaps Dante had got lost or fallen into a quarry or something. I did not know the area as we had actually crossed over into a neighbouring Force's patch.

I decided to call Dante back. I called him about three times and eventually I could hear him panting and crashing through the undergrowth coming back to me. When he got back to me he spun around and ran back into the bushes, not giving me time to put him back onto his lead. I thought to myself – I know what that means, he's still onto something. I called him back to me and put his harness and line back on.

This time we both pushed through the undergrowth and to my amazement the bushes opened out and we went down an embankment onto a woodland pathway. The pathway was more like a stream at this point as the rain was so heavy it was running off the embankment and pouring along the path, but this didn't put Dante off.

We tracked along the path, in the darkness for about half a mile, then Dante turned right and went through some undergrowth and came out on a single track road. He then tracked down the road for quite a way, every now and then heading up the banking to the right and then coming back down on to the road. At one point he crossed over the lane, went up the banking and weaved in and out of the trees, hesitating now and then. He lifted his head every so often to sniff the air, but quickly put his nose down again and continued to track down the lane.

At the bottom of the lane there was a forestry gateway where horse riders could gain access to the woods. Dante went over this gateway and we appeared to be going around in circles. I thought to myself that he had lost the track or perhaps someone had picked the man up in a car and driven off. By this time some of the traffic unit officers had driven down the lane and were parked at the bottom near the forestry entrance. I felt so embarrassed wondering what they must be thinking of me and my dog having reached this far and losing it!

I decided to let Dante search again without the hindrance

of having to pull me behind him. I left his harness on but unclipped the line and I shouted my usual challenge again, and let him go. I watched him closely and saw him work hard to find the track again. Then I saw the change. The same change in his demeanour I had seen many times before when he was onto something. To my surprise he came straight towards me, back the way we had tracked down the lane.

As he went to run past me I called him to me and clipped the line back onto his harness. We tracked again together back up the lane the way we had come, heading towards a traffic car that was driving slowly towards us. Dante paid no attention to the car and ran straight past it and continued up the road. After about 150 metres Dante went up the embankment to the left. Here he pushed through thick undergrowth, leaving me to follow. Then he started to bark, he had found the male hiding in thick bushes lying down flat on the floor.

The ill advised young man kicked out at Dante who then took great pleasure in biting him on the leg and arm in retaliation and self-defence. The male was arrested for the theft of the vehicle, which was originally from the Machen area, and handed over to Gwent officers who by this time had also arrived at the scene.

I was overjoyed. Dante and I were exhausted, soaked through to the skin, cut to bits by blackberries but the happiest dog team in South Wales Police.

Bizarre Stories

The dog teams from South Wales Police are tasked to many different operations throughout their area and beyond. No two operations are the same, many are unusual and occasionally some evolve into quite bizarre stories of extraordinary behaviour. The tales in this chapter have little to bind them together other than they all provide a very good story, sufficiently unusual to be labelled bizarre.

PC Mark Frowen

It is not unusual to find dog lovers in the course of my work but it is very unusual to find someone whom my dog has been chasing, intent on restraining or even biting him, who loves dogs sufficiently to risk their own life for the safety of the dog. This story happened to me in November 2009 when I and my dog Jack were sent up the Little Rhondda Valley to the small town of Tylorstown where some youths had evaded capture by local divisional officers after being involved in a burglary.

The youths had all headed south down the valley towards the town of Porth where the tributary joins the main Rhondda River. Here they had separated, some choosing to dodge the traffic on the busy Porth bypass where I could not possibly release Jack to pursue them.

However I spotted one youth heading away from the road towards some waste ground running alongside the very fast flowing and flooded River Rhondda. I decided to follow him, so drove the van as close as I could get before releasing Jack in pursuit.

Jack chased after the young man and was gaining on him when the boy decided the only escape route was to jump into the river; without hesitation Jack followed. They both flew down the river but the boy was obviously a very strong swimmer and soon I could see he was safe on the other bank. At this stage I thought I had lost Jack for good.

I chased down my side of the river until I was right opposite the youth, who was running to keep alongside Jack as the current swept him downstream. "Shall I go back in after him?" the youth shouted across at me. "No", I told him, "stay exactly where you are" as I did not want his death on my conscience as well.

But I should have had more faith in Jack who somehow now made the other bank and, despite having very nearly drowned, had not lost his focus on the job in hand. Having had a quick shake he ran back upriver to where the youth was standing and bit him on the leg! There was not much I could do to stop him but, having instructed Jack to release him, I told our now rather sore fugitive to climb a nearby tree and wait until I could get to him. I legged it back to the van, drove it over the bridge and down to where the pair of them awaited my arrival. Neither had moved.

I arrested the young man on suspicion of burglary and, having towelled Jack down, put my dog back in his cage. I felt rather sorry for our prisoner, as he had been prepared to risk his own life to save that of my dog. I hope it counted for him when he came in front of the magistrate.

Another extraordinary tale of a dog-loving criminal also took place in the Rhondda Valley. Some officers in Tonyrefail had put out a call for urgent assistance and when I arrived there it was to a rather bizarre sight. One officer had detained a suspect and was sitting in the police car with him while the other officer was being chased around a skip by a man with a large kitchen knife.

I jumped out of the van with my dog Ben and headed towards the skip, passing right by the police car. As we passed the car the prisoner inside somehow managed to get out and was aggressively yelling, whilst flailing his arms wildly at me: "You want to get him, he'll kill him otherwise". Unfortunately Ben did not appreciate that this shouting man was just providing a warning and immediately perceived this as a threat to me so growled fiercely at the man to ensure he came no nearer. This took a few seconds to unravel before I could turn my attention back to the man with the knife.

At this stage he stopped chasing my divisional colleague round the skip, turned his attention to me and announced, "I don't want to hurt your dog, I just want to stab you". I deployed Ben who straight away attacked his right arm, having appreciated that the knife was in his right hand. Despite his blood spouting everywhere the man still did not drop the knife. While Ben continued to bite his right arm he reached inside his jacket with his left hand and pulled out another kitchen knife. He then proceeded towards me dragging 34 kilos of Ben along beside him. He seemed to feel no pain and certainly did not attempt to attack Ben with the knife in his free hand, with which he could easily have killed him.

As he drew up alongside the police car he put both knives down on the bonnet and gave himself up. After he had been handcuffed and arrested he announced that he would never have hurt the dog, he just wanted to stab a police officer!

High above Tylorstown on the eastern side of the valley is St Gwynno Forest, an attractive wooded area with waterfalls, glades and lovely forest rides and tracks, much used at weekends by people who want to enjoy long walks in glorious countryside. However in mid-winter and in mid-week it is a very remote spot, ideal for discreetly stripping down a stolen car.

It was just such a crime to which I was despatched with my dog Ben. Someone had spotted two men behaving suspiciously only a short time before, but the men had obviously realised they had been rumbled, had taken flight and decided to abandon the car to avoid being caught. But, as there were few people about, it was not difficult for Ben to pick up a scent and very shortly we were off tracking down a ride towards the small town of Ferndale to the north west.

Ben was pulling me along at a fair old pace and I soon spotted them about half a mile ahead of us, which was a long gap to close. Then suddenly we came across three girls out riding. I stopped them and asked whether I might borrow one of their horses to aid my pursuit. They thought this was a tremendous joke, thinking no doubt they would watch this copper being thrown off within a few yards of setting off. But they were very happy to lend me one of their steeds and off I set at a canter with Ben running beside me.

Being reasonably competent on a horse it did not take long before I had caught up with the two men and with Ben's help I handcuffed and arrested them. Unfortunately I had forgotten Ben's antipathy to horses and as we came to a stop Ben forgot that the men were his quarry and sank his teeth into the backside of the horse. It certainly provided an incentive for our two fugitives not to be the subject of Ben's displeasure.

Having returned the horse to its owner I then had to apologise profusely and arrange for treatment by a vet. But just like the US Rangers – we got our man.

PS John Codd

This incident took place over 20 years ago: A different era of policing compared to the challenges of today, one reminiscent of 'Heartbeat', when officers and criminals often knew one another's strengths and weaknesses and played a mutually respectful game of cat and mouse.

When a dog section police officer goes on holiday it is normal practice to drop his dog off at the training kennels at Waterton Cross, Bridgend, where the dog will be well looked after by the staff there. I was about to depart on my annual leave and had arranged for another handler to pick up both me and my dog Jas so I could drop him off at the kennels. I was in civilian clothes without any kit, not even a lead.

While we were en-route a call came over the radio of my colleague, Dai, about an abandoned stolen vehicle that was only just off our route to Waterton. We decided to go and have a look at it. On arrival Dai got his dog out, put him in a harness and soon it was very evident that he had a good scent on which to track. Before he set off we had agreed that this would allow me to give Jas a good walk while we were waiting, so Dai locked the van and headed off.

Jas and I set off on our leisurely walk in the adjacent fields and we had only gone a short distance when I noticed Jas's behaviour and body language had taken on that familiar 'back to work' mode; I knew at once he had found something. He started to track off in the opposite direction to Dai, but I knew my dog and knew to follow him.

Without a lead to restrain him I struggled to keep up as we travelled for nearly a mile. He then stopped suddenly, turned to the right and dived into the bushes barking vociferously, indicating he had found our man. We had found our thief but, without handcuffs or a radio, I was rather limited in my options. So I ordered the man to get up and we escorted him all the way back to the van, which of course was still locked and there was no sign of Dai anywhere. Frustratingly I could see the radio in the van but had no way of getting at it. Then I remembered that beside me was a professional car thief. So I turned to him and asked: "Any chance you could break into the van without causing any damage?" So he obliged. I could then contact the control room and Dai, who was miles away on the other side of a mountain. Eventually my man was arrested and taken into custody. Jas and I could both now go on our individual annual leaves.

PC Paul Krauze

It was 5 a.m. on a really cold winter's morning and it had been snowing all night. I was leaving Cocket police station in Swansea after dealing with a prisoner and was heading home, together with my dog King who was in the back of the van fast asleep.

A short distance from the station, I came to a stop as the road was blocked by two rabbits, one in either lane. I drove quite close, I flashed my lights and I beeped the horn but they wouldn't move. I got out of the vehicle and tried to shoo them away but they still wouldn't budge. By now about 10 minutes had passed so I called my sergeant to come and take a look. (He thought I was having issues getting King back into the van as quite often happened because he could be a grumpy old fellow).

I returned to my car and put on my issued black leather gloves and went to pick them up just as my sergeant pulled up behind me. I grabbed one by its ears and put my other hand under its bum, just as I had seen on TV, and carried it carefully to the kerb. It didn't struggle at all.

As I placed it back down, it suddenly went berserk. It was jumping up at my legs and biting my hands and trousers. At that point the other rabbit came bounding over and joined in the attack! I had to run to my van just to get away from them only to see the sergeant still sat in his van, weak with laughter.

I was out looking for a stolen vehicle in the Rhyd y Pandy area north of Swansea. It was a night shift and it was very, very misty with very poor visibility. On board I had my dog King. A short while later a colleague in another car managed to find the stolen vehicle and he began to pursue it, all the time sending observations and directions as to where they were. After about 20 minutes I thought I knew where it was heading and made my way up on to the mountain road.

My fellow officer said that he had lost sight of it and it had gone over the mountain. Then suddenly it came off the mountainside, across the road in front of me and carried on down the side of the hill, just like in the movies. I stopped my car in shock and then realised that the vehicle must have hit something that had brought it to a halt, as I could no longer hear it moving. I quickly got out of the car with King and sent him to locate the vehicle occupants.

A short while later I heard the screams and knew that King had found them, so I started running towards the sound. King had located four men and as I was trying to sort out the mêlée, I realised that there was another dog there. What I didn't realise was that my colleague had come over the mountain in the mist behind the stolen vehicle, seen my car and was so annoyed that I was going to get his prisoners, he had sent his dog as well!

As we both got the four men back to the police vans, we were met by a divisional traffic officer who said, "Two dogs? Two dogs? You lot are like buses – I tried to get a dog last week to no avail and now I get two!"

PC Mike Newman

One of the possible perks of our job is that we occasionally get to go to popular events which would otherwise cost a small fortune to attend – the rugby internationals, football matches and the occasional concert or music festival. One summer I and my drugs dog Bailey were tasked to work at 'Escape to the Park', a major music festival in Swansea. A condition of entry for all ticket holders was that they must consent to being searched for alcohol and drugs. Bailey was a passive trained drugs detection dog and would indicate if someone had drugs by sitting down beside them.

As you can imagine we had seen some fairly strange sights during the course of the day, including every type of fashion worn by people from every age group and social class. Many came with camping gear and with provisions for themselves and sometimes for their children or even babies. We had had a lot of fun as they traipsed past us. Although we had found the odd bottle of alcohol (which we would confiscate and hand over to the organisers!) we had not found anyone trying to smuggle in drugs. They all knew the score and respected the search dogs too much to try it on.

But then all of a sudden Bailey went and sat down beside a woman of a large frame who was only wearing a bikini top and very small shorts. Bailey's actions seemed very strange as there really did not seem to be anywhere on her person in which to conceal drugs.

But I trusted Bailey so I called over two female officers who took the lady away to be searched more discreetly in a tent. One of the first things they did was to invite her to 'lift up' her very large breasts. Underneath they found 600 ecstasy tablets, all ready for distribution. This would certainly have paid for her ticket. She never did get to hear the music, just faced another type of music with the magistrate the next day.

Police Humour

Police work at times can be full of tedium: perhaps hours on patrol with absolutely nothing of any interest happening anywhere in the district; or sitting in an office dealing with mountains of routine paperwork; or spending the whole shift sitting in a police station or a van waiting for an operation to be triggered – only for it to be cancelled. Likewise police work can be exceedingly unpleasant with many gruesome scenes or disagreeable people to deal with, or it can be incredibly exciting or even very frightening.

Throughout all this the officers of South Wales Police have to maintain a sense of balance and, not least important when dealing with the public, a robust sense of humour. Sometimes, particularly amongst themselves, the humour may be somewhat unique but humour plays a huge part in ensuring that all the stresses of operational work do not result in problems of the mind, which might impinge on officers' approach to their work or threaten their mental health.

When the South Wales Police were sent to assist the Metropolitan Police during the riots of 2011, Londoners were particularly impressed with the wit and humour that was deployed with them even if the broad Welsh accent did not always help in understanding what was being said. It certainly helped resolve many a difficult moment with confrontational youths from some of the more challenging areas of London.

PC Bob Woolford

Before I became a dog handler I had walked the beat for some years in the small town of Neath. I had always prided myself on my appearance, ensuring my boots were always the shiniest on the shift and that my uniform was always immaculately pressed. I saw no reason that, having now qualified to be part of the Dog Section, that I should change the habits of a lifetime.

So, on my very first day in the Section, I had ensured that my appearance was immaculate before setting out to exercise my dogs on the way in to work. I had recently moved home to a village where one of my new colleagues, PS John Codd, also happened to live. He had very kindly advised me about the local area and where best to exercise dogs. Therefore, having made my way to one of those fields, it was no surprise to find him and his van, having just finished exercising all his charges.

We had a quick chat and then John turned back to his van, opened the doors and out jumped six of the muddiest Mutts imaginable. They all pounced on me determined to greet me and welcome me personally to this new area. They were particularly excited as they thought they were about to get a second lot of exercise. I looked down at my uniform, which was now covered with mud and saliva from top to not-so-shiniest toe. And I had not even started my shift yet.

John called his dogs back into the van and turned back to me chuckling to say: "Welcome to the Dog Section, Bob. Now you look like a proper dog handler!"

My very first dog was a long-haired, German Shepherd called Simba. While we were both undergoing initial training I spent much time grooming Simba, ensuring that his lovely sable coloured coat was always immaculately clean and in the very best condition. I like to think that if there had ever been a prize for the best turned-out dog, Simba would have won it on every day of the course.

The course was also great fun for us all. We were all experienced coppers learning a new skill and we had great fun together. There was much banter between us, many jokes and even the odd trick played against either students or instructors.

One morning we were told just before going to lunch that in the afternoon we would be doing environmental training, which involved walking our dogs in and around Bridgend town centre. So, after our lunch, I grabbed a lead and headed off to the kennels to get Simba.

I made my way down the row of kennels and there, half way along the row, all excited and ready to greet me, was Simba. But not my beautiful, sable coloured, immaculately groomed dog but now a lurid pink one that looked more like a punk rocker. Behind me I heard a snigger and there, at the end of the kennel block, was the entire course who were all doubled up with laughter.

Desperate not to give them the reaction they were seeking, I unlocked the kennel, put Simba on his lead and brought him out. With as much dignity as I could muster, I informed the instructor, who was close to doing himself an injury from his suppressed giggling, that I would not be participating in the environmental training that afternoon. Leaving my colleagues still in paroxysms of mirth, I took Simba to the grooming area where I spent the rest of the afternoon washing out the otherwise harmless pink vegetable dye from his coat. Simba was not complaining, he enjoyed his grooming sessions enormously and he really had no idea about his part in the joke.

I was deployed on a very boring operation with some divisional officers, one of whom had been winding up my dog Todd.

After a while I asked him to desist or I would let Todd off his lead and then let the dog sort him out. The officer obviously did not believe me and continued his teasing, getting the dog really irritated and causing me to have to hold him back quite vigorously.

After a while we were both totally fed up with his goading, so I decided that the officer was close enough to his car that if he moved sufficiently quickly he would be quite safe inside it. So very loudly I said: "Go on, run!" and, giving him sufficient head start, I released Todd as the copper legged it back into his car.

Fortunately for him it was not locked and he made it, just, into the driver's seat where with the doors locked and the window up he continued to bate Todd. Frustrated by all this, Todd decided that if he could not actually get at his tormentor he could at least stop him going anywhere. So he went to the front of the car and bit into the front tyre, which started to deflate almost at once. Within seconds it was flat as a pancake. I am not quite sure how the officer explained that in his report.

PC Gareth Jones

I was leaving home and about to clock on for a night shift when I heard on the radio about an alarm going off at a mansion, just two minutes up the road from my house. So I sped up there and was the first to arrive. I got my dog Max out of the van and together we walked round, looking for any signs of forced entry.

At the back we found a kitchen door open, which we found led to a long corridor with many rooms leading off it. So standing in the doorway I challenged loudly for anyone inside to come out and show themselves. There was no reply so I unleashed Max and let him go in to have a good look.

He started to work his way through the darkened rooms

when suddenly a light came on in one of them and I heard a voice saying: "Morning Master". I jumped with shock. Max left the room and the light went off. I called him back but he went back in again, once more the light came on and the same voice called out the same greeting.

With that I yelled the command "Hold him!" so that Max would grab whoever it was in there mucking us about. I followed down the corridor, all the while hearing the same voice saying: "Morning master" and I continued yelling: "Hold him, hold him!"

As I turned into the room I found Max sitting transfixed in the middle of the room, staring at a wall mounted figure-head, from which this voice was emanating. I really had made a bit of a fool of myself but still thank goodness, I thought, there was no-one to witness it.

I turned round to go out and there was a local officer who knew me well, doubled up in pain from suppressing his laughter. No, I was not allowed to get away with it.

Life has its Ups and Downs

All police dog handlers will have incidents that will remain in their minds for the rest of their lives. Certainly this incident required no reference to any notes of evidence for total recall even years after it happened.

PC Alan Russ

I'd been a police officer for twenty years and a dog handler for seven. Over that time I had worked with three General Purpose dogs, but Chase was always my favourite. We came together as a team purely by accident. My previous dog had retired early and Chase had been donated by a member of the public unable to control this boisterous fur ball.

Chase was a long haired German Shepherd, sort of light beige in colour and quite the most handsome dog you could ever imagine. That said, he was a big boy, weighing in at 32kg (ie about 5 stones or half a human). Chase was wonderful with my family and had lived with us now for five years. He adored both my two kids and my wife. However, as soon as I put my uniform on, he would change from a playful, mischievous youth to a dedicated partner. Like most police dogs and horses he seemed to know his role in life. Put simply – to serve and protect.

I thought I had seen everything there was to see that the job could throw at me. How wrong can you be? I'll never forget that night in 1996. It started off perfectly normal: a typical mid-week night shift you could say. There had been the usual good-natured, light-hearted banter typical of any police station before setting off. It was raining. I settled myself in for a night of humdrum activity coupled with the odd interjection of boredom. How wrong was I!

Suddenly a call came over the radio to say that a female police officer had disturbed two suspects breaking into a furniture store. She was in pursuit on foot and both she and the suspects were heading down the same road that I was travelling on. Luck was on our side – this was going to be a good night.

No sooner had I smiled to myself and put the lights and siren on than the two suspects suddenly appeared in my headlights. I honestly don't know who was most surprised, me for them landing in my lap or them for being the unluckiest villains in Wales.

I stopped the van and immediately jumped out. In typical fashion the two would-be burglars turned and ran. I raced around to the back of the van and shouted 'Police Dog Stop'. This of course made no difference except possibly to make the two lads run even faster. Immediately I released Chase and, true to his name, he was off like an Exocet missile. I jogged along behind, letting him do the work (and me take the credit)! Within seconds I heard that sound so familiar to all police dog handlers – a human being whimpering. I got to the scene shortly and there was Chase detaining the first suspect. Quickly, I got him to release the guy and as luck would have it my colleague caught up with us. I handcuffed the miscreant and left him in her custody.

I turned back to my dog. I could not believe my eyes, Chase, my faithful partner was gone. The thrill of the chase was too much for him and instead of waiting for my command he was off in pursuit of the second suspect without any instruction from me. I felt completely redundant and pondered that if they ever got dogs to drive, I could be out of a job.

I shouted and shouted, but nothing – so I set off along the track in the only direction my errant canine partner could have gone. I was cursing him for a sudden streak of disobedience, proud of him for showing such commitment and panicking quietly that I might not get him back for hours. That would take some explaining and some mickey taking for months to come. All these thoughts going through my mind and it was still raining!

Suddenly there was the sound of wood cracking and as I rounded a corner I was met with a sight in the distance that beggared belief. My mind simply could not compute it. There was Chase latched on to the leg of the remaining suspect, who was straddled across the top of a tall fence. Nothing strange in that but what came next was incredible.

The suspect who was a slightly built young man, suddenly, with what appeared to be a feat of superhuman strength, lifted himself over the fence and took Chase skywards. Chase was completely off the ground with his feet firmly on the fence. I am sure in the moonlight I saw his eyes widen in disbelief. Again there was that sound of wood cracking and I feared the worst.

To lift a 5 stone German Shepherd off the ground normally takes some strength, but to do it with one clamped to your ankle is unbelievable. As I ran towards them the thought went through my mind that if he was that strong then perhaps I had better radio for back up as even Chase and I together could have problems with this guy. I am so, so glad I never made that call.

Chase was by this time angry and in a fit of snarling rage dragged the suspect back over the fence. Seconds later, the guy was at it again. He lifted Chase clean off the ground. I ran as fast as I could to give Chase some urgent help, only to see him valiantly drag the suspect back to our side of the fence again.

It then became clear as to why Chase and the suspect had been in a see-saw motion backwards and forwards over the fence. Unbeknownst to Chase and me, there were two other police officers the other side of the fence pulling the suspect over! Chase had clamped on his leg and simply was not going to give up his prize.

How the other officers did not laugh (although I think playing tug of war with a very angry German Shepherd for a few minutes may have had something to do with it) I will never know. We arrested the suspect and escorted him back to the Panda car. When I got back from patrol it brought a great smile to everyone at the nick and certainly raised a few spirits among those whose evenings had been less entertaining.

Chase has now sadly passed away. We will never forget

him, even though every dog I had partnered has been equally special. The family miss him, but we never did let him play see-saw or tug of war with the kids – you see he was too good at it for two fully grown Bobbies to beat!

I still have the best job in the world though.

A Hero's Tail

176

Dante's Triumph

During a career in the Dog Section police officers may well handle a number of dogs whose whole lives will be spent with them as their working partners and often, eventually in retirement, as pets in their homes. During all that time they become as close as if they were part of their family.

All those who have had dogs as pets will be aware how close a relationship is formed. But police dogs will have worked with their handlers in some very testing and often very dangerous operational situations, sometimes the dogs will have saved their handlers from getting seriously hurt or even have saved their lives. A police dog and its handler have to have implicit trust in each other, this makes that bond even stronger.

PC Sam Dunstan

What a lot of people don't realise is that joining the Police gives you the opportunity to follow many different career paths: specialist search and rescue, traffic, air support, firearms, family liaison or CID to name but a few. If you find a job doesn't suit you, unlike in conventional career paths, you don't have to change employer, just change your role. With so many diverse specialisations there really is something for everyone.

It was the autumn of 1999. I had been a police officer for seven years and with the dawning of the new millennium I too felt ready for a change and my family knew it. I had always loved animals when growing up. Knowing that my family encouraged me to apply to become a dog handler – how clever were they! My enthusiasm for both the animals and the role must have shone through because I was successful in my application to join the South Wales Police Dog and Mounted Section.

My love of horses also helped and later I was to become a reserve rider for the Mounted Team. Jobs don't come any better than this, but at the same time, sadly they don't come much worse on occasions.

My first dog was called Ben. He was a mountain of a German Shepherd, short-haired and really a lovely dog. In fact, he was too lovely. I worked hard with him for a number of years and a more loyal companion you could not get. Unfortunately though, Ben's heart wasn't in the job and as time wore on you could see his reluctance to do what was expected of him. At times like these, you have to put the animal first; your own feelings don't matter.

Eventually I and my Sergeant, who had been hugely supportive throughout this difficult time, took the decision to chop Ben. 'Chopped' isn't quite as bad as it sounds. It is the term used when a dog or a horse fails to make the grade for police work and is therefore removed from service. In Ben's case this meant him being rehomed as a pet. He went to live with a lovely family, I even vetted them myself and when I visited them six months later to check how Ben was doing, I realised how right the decision had been. He was loving life, playing with the family's three children and sleeping with the cat!

It was now autumn 2005 and my Sergeant, who had been brilliant during all this, asked me to re-handle an old dog called Dante. I was not very happy about this as I felt the dog was only going to last a couple of years and then I was going to have to go through the same process again. After several discussions, and with a great deal of reluctance on my part, I followed my Sergeant's advice and agreed to become Dante's handler.

When I think back to that cold, wet autumn day walking into the kennels at Waterton Cross, Bridgend and seeing a bony, moth-eaten, big-eared, massive-pawed elderly German Shepherd, little did I know that this dog would be my teacher, my protector, but most of all my truest friend. How little did I know that my alliance with Dante would be the most spectacular of my career to date?

It was not long after our re-handle course that Dante showed me exactly what he was capable of. Traffic units had followed a stolen motorcycle across the Ely area of Cardiff and had lost sight of it near to parkland. The traffic officers believed that it had made off into woodland nearby. They asked for a dog handler to attend and as Dante and I had just started our night shift at 7 p.m., we made our way to Ely.

When we arrived a short time later, the traffic officers explained to me that they believed the motorbike thief was hiding in the wooded area. I deployed Dante from the van and we made a search of the area that the officers had directed us to. It was a beautiful evening, early autumn, and it was warm as the sun was just starting to go down. After about half an hour of searching, all the traffic officers had lost interest and I started to wind down my search. Dante was off his lead and was sniffing around in the bushes and undergrowth searching. I was totally convinced that the motorcycle and its thief had long gone, but not Dante.

"Dante, come! Dante, COME!!" I shouted, but the usually superbly obedient Dante had decided to completely ignore my commands! A little bit taken aback at his defiance, I called him again, only this time a little more firmly and eventually I saw him coming back towards me. My firmness was interrupted by my radio sounding a relentless beeping; someone was trying to contact me. I answered the caller and we struck up a conversation.

The conversation was completely one-sided as I listened

to him ramble on. As he talked, I watched Dante closely. His body language and posture had completely changed. He went from a methodical search to frantic, head down, nose to the ground in tracking mode. "Sorry mate, got to cut you off, Dante's got something", came my eventual reply.

As I watched Dante, still nose to the ground, he loped across the muddy pathway into the darkening wood. I ran as fast as I could behind him and watched in amazement as he free-tracked, left and right, through the woods. This time I recalled him and put him on his lead.

By now the light had started to fade and the woodland was almost dark. Instinct told me to trust this dog and that Dante was onto something. As I looked into the distance I saw a tiny red light about 100 metres away. By now Dante was pulling on the lead, still with his nose to the ground and he was letting out a periodic high pitched squeak that he made in frustration and excitement when he was on the scent of a criminal. We started to run; I kept my eyes fixed on the red light and Dante kept his nose on the ground.

At first I thought the light might have been a cigarette tip burning in the distance, perhaps being smoked by some innocent member of the public out for an evening stroll in the woods (about to get the shock of their lives). However as we jogged closer I saw exactly what it was. It was the motorbike thief pushing the stolen bike through the woods trying to make good his escape. The tail light on the bike was still switched on.

Dante and I jogged towards him, trying to close the gap before he saw us. My heart was thumping in my chest as we got closer and closer. Dante lifted his head and his eyes locked on to the thief, who was still unaware that we were on to him.

As we got closer, the thief turned and saw us. He threw down the bike and was off on his toes through the trees. I yelled out, "Police Dog, stay where you are!" This was quickly followed by "Hold him" which is the command for the dog to chase and detain the male by biting him.

I slipped the chain from Dante's neck and he shot like a missile through the trees after our man. This was the very first time I had deployed Dante for a 'chase and detain' for real! He had always performed perfectly in training, however experience had taught me that it was one thing to do it in training, but a completely different kettle of fish when the 'fugitive' wasn't just acting as a criminal and wearing a protective sleeve. Dante disappeared into the gloom and for a split second I lost sight of him. Then I heard the screams.

Dante had caught him, taking him by the right arm (as per his training) and they had fallen to the ground. A struggle was taking place with our fugitive kicking out at Dante, trying to escape. During this struggle he was bitten several times on his legs and abdomen. I ran as fast as I could, and on seeing that

Dante had caught our man, I quickly called him off, arrested the man and handcuffed him.

I was so proud of my boy: his steely determination, when his handler had given up and was ready to go back to the van; his obedience in allowing me to recall him when he was so focussed on a track and his bravery when taking on the bad guy. This was one of the first jobs we did together as an operational dog team, one of the many successful encounters we were to have over the next three years. During our time together we were nominated for 'Police Officer of the Year' in recognition of our success. To me it was a nomination in recognition of a very special relationship.

During the summer of 2007 Dante's age began to show. He became weak and could no longer keep up the pace of a police dog's life. He retired in August 2007 and there was no choice other than to become my much-loved family pet. My family all adored him. Quite unexpectedly, Dante adapted to family life very well. He loved a game of catch and to play ball with the kids. As long as I took him with me on night shifts with the operational dogs he was happy.

The joy we all felt at having Dante in our lives was sadly to be cut short. On May 24th 2008 at 3.00 p.m. Dante suffered a stroke and lost the use of his back legs. I drove to my vets fighting back the tears and, as I carried him into the vets, I already knew that this was the end. I looked into his eyes and felt his pain. I knew I had to make the most difficult decision.

I sat down on the floor of the vet's consulting room and cradled his head in my lap, stroked his beautiful long ears and told him how brave he was, how much he would be missed and how grateful I was to have had him as my teacher, my protector and my truest friend.

Then I had to let him go.

As I sat there on the floor with tears streaming down my face, I knew I was blessed to have known such a wonderful animal and to have had a unique and special bond with a very special dog.

The pain of losing him was unbearable. For months something would bring back a memory and it would be all I could do to hold back my tears.

Nothing could replace my Dante.

This is why I said jobs don't come much better than this, but sadly, on occasions they don't come much worse. As a dog handler our canine partners don't live for a relatively long period. Someone once said that to love a dog is the most rewarding thing in the world but at the same time the most heart breaking, for they are with us for such a short time. How our friends at Wood Green and at Dogs Trust cope with their jobs beggars belief. It is only the joy of the friendship of a dog that wins through in the end.

To this day I feel Dante's presence when out on an operation. He really was, and always will be, my teacher, my protector, but most of all, my truest friend. I will always miss him, forever remember him and never forget that your Sergeant knows best!

Dante's poem

Countless are the times, dear friend …
You saved me.
Unrivalled, undaunted, bold.
Undying devotion through the darkness
Enviable loyalty, undeniable determination
You carried me with you
Each adventure our own
Always watching, always ready, always my rock.
And now at the end of days,
Now all is done
And no more can I ask
I vow that at your passing
For you, no pain... dear friend
The dignity you earned in life
I promised at your end.
And as in life you carried me
Now I shall carry you
You were my very heart and soul
Thief taker... friend... and true.

For Dante 1998-2008 RIP

The End... for now

Epilogue

I have been asked to write this epilogue to explain why and how Wood Green, The Animals Charity became involved with "A Hero's Tail" project and the production of this book.

Looking back, I think my personal interest and commitment to this project dates back to my service in the Royal Air Force, when I often worked with the RAF Police and their dogs. In fact, in 1983 I rehomed two RAF "sniffer dogs". Both were golden retrievers who, unfortunately, failed their training. Olma, the bitch, was a bit too fussy about who she met, while Baxter the dog was thought not to be clever enough. Actually, I think he was too clever. He enjoyed the training games, but there was no way he was going to work for a living!

Then, in 1988, I was posted to RAF Wittering – the "Home of the Harrier" on the A1 near Stamford. There, I commanded the Wing that provided all the base support to the flying operations, which included command of the RAF Police and their dogs. I loved those dogs and my children and I would often visit the kennels when the dogs were off-duty and play with those big German Shepherds. However, on-duty these dogs were very different, as I found out when I donned the padded suit for a training experience and was captured very quickly by Air Dog Sabre. Aware of the professionalism of the dogs and their handlers, I knew what to expect. However, for the average villain with no such knowledge, being arrested by a five stone German Shepherd must be a pretty frightening experience.

In 2000, I decided to take early retirement from the Royal Air Force and was offered the post of Chief Executive at Wood Green. The Charity was well-known, rehoming a range of animals from hamsters up to horses, but mainly cats and dogs. However in the 1990s, it had suffered some hard times and needed revitalising. It was clear from the onset that Wood Green employed some brilliant people; dedicated, knowledgeable and utterly committed to the welfare of animals in their care. Unfortunately, the facilities at Wood Green's three centres were outdated, well past their best and did not offer the right kind of environment to provide the animals with the stimulus they needed to keep them happy and content until such time as we could find them new, loving homes.

Consequently, we set about increasing our income through a number of modern fundraising schemes and keeping in close contact with all our supporters to ensure they all felt part of the Wood Green family. In addition, our 52 acre site at King's Bush Farm, north of Cambridge, is one of the biggest rehoming centres in Europe and a major visitor centre in Cambridgeshire. With an Olympic size equestrian arena and a 300 seat restaurant, we could hold a range of events including pop concerts, dog and cat shows and silver service dinners. In fact, we have a wedding licence so that people can get married with (but not to!) their pets. We also had one of the first wind turbines in the UK, which was installed in 1990. With increased income from fundraising and trading, and with some significant legacies, we were able to rebuild or update the facilities and to incorporate some innovative details to improve the quality of life for the animals during their stay with us.

I first met Matthew Rees, the Veterinary Director of Technik Technology, at an animal welfare conference in 2007. His company makes stainless steel veterinary equipment and had been doing some work for the Dogs Trust designing and manufacturing their new kennels. I was interested in his work because Wood Green intended to replace its veterinary surgery and intake kennels, as and when funds become available. Over the years, we kept in touch and became good friends.

In 2010, Wood Green started detailed planning for new surgery and kennel buildings and brought Matthew and his team on board to help with the design. At that time, he had to liaise with our dog welfare staff and was clearly impressed with their knowledge and skills. I knew Matthew's wife Sian, was, like my wife, into horses, but I then discovered that she voluntarily provided a rest and recuperation facility for the police horses of the South Wales Police.

Matthew and Sian often visited the South Wales Police Dog and Mounted Sections at Waterton, Bridgend. During their visits, Matthew became increasingly aware that, although the police dogs were cared for very attentively by staff, their basic kennels were in need of substantial repair and modernisation. It was obvious that they were loved by their handlers and well looked after, but the kennels at Waterton were old and greatly in need of refurbishment or, better still, replacement. Certainly, the kennels were in a far worse condition than those at the many animal welfare charities Matthew had visited. Unfortunately, in this period of austerity, there was limited money available in the Chief Constable's budget to spend on the police dog kennels.

Consequently, knowing Wood Green's reputation for innovation and high standards of dog welfare, Matthew came to see me to ask if there was anything Wood Green could do to help the South Wales Police dogs. The first thing I did was to dispatch two senior members of our dog staff, Sue Ketland and Emma Jeffery to Waterton to view the facilities. Sue is our Behaviour and Training Manager and Emma is a German Shepherd specialist. Both are very knowledgeable about each dog breed's behaviour patterns and what can be done to enrich their kennel space so that dogs can have a happy, contented downtime when not working.

When Sue and Emma returned to Wood Green they were sad. They had seen some wonderful working dogs, each with an important role in protecting the public, but they lived in conditions, which, although quite adequate in basic terms, with investment could have been so very much better. This was what these brave, loyal and hardworking dogs deserved. They made it clear to me, in no uncertain terms, that we had to do something. As always, "doing something" meant finding money and in this case to raise funds to improve the facilities for these dogs.

Clearly, we could not use the money donated to Wood Green, so we had to come up with an innovative (that word again!) scheme to raise funds to rebuild the kennels. After much discussion, it became obvious to me that the best promoters of any scheme were the dogs themselves and the work they do. At the same time, many of the dog handlers told us stories about their dogs; some funny, some sad, but all interesting. From this came the idea of bringing the stories together into a book.

Getting from that idea to a published book took a lot of hard work by some dedicated people, but, most importantly, you bought the book! I hope you enjoyed the stories and are buoyed by the thought that the profits from this book will go to improve the welfare of the South Wales Police dogs whose sole job is to protect us, the public.

Group Captain Dennis Baker OBE

A Debt of Gratitude

This book could not have been published without the following companies' fantastic support:

Agria Pet Insurance
All Things Wild, Honeybourne
Canon Ltd
Cardiff Castle
Centaur Veterinary Services Ltd
Ceva Animal Health
Glamorgan County Cricket
Loop Concepts
Miele Ltd
Safe Solutions
Technik Technology Ltd
The London Vet Show
The Spirit of Pegasus
Veterinary X-Rays
Vet Index Publications
W&H (UK Ltd)
Welsh Rugby Union
Worldwide Veterinary Service

Additionally a large thank you is due to all those people who undertook different sponsored events to help raise funds for this project.

To PC Ian Squire and all the team at Durham Constabulary Dog Section and their initiative Paws Up, we wish you the greatest success.